1,500
GREAT
Gift
IDEAS

1,500 GREAT

Gift

IDEAS

Lorraine Bodger

**Andrews McMeel
Publishing**

Kansas City

03 04 05 06 07 KFO 10 9 8 7 6 5 4 3 2 1

Library of Congress Cataloging-in-Publication Data

Bodger, Lorraine
    1,500 great gift ideas / Lorraine Bodger.
        p. cm.
    ISBN 0-7407-3820-8
    1. Gifts. I. Title: One thousand five hundred great gift ideas. II. Title.

    GT3040.B63 2003
    394—dc21   2003050338

Illustrations by Lorraine Bodger
Book design by Lisa Martin

ATTENTION: SCHOOLS AND BUSINESSES
Andrews McMeel books are available at quantity discounts with bulk purchase for educational, business, or sales promotional use. For information, please write to: Special Sales Department, Andrews McMeel Publishing, 4520 Main Street, Kansas City, Missouri 64111.

Contents

CONTENTS

CONTENTS

Extras

1,500 GREAT GIFT IDEAS

Introduction

You're standing in the mall, scratching your head. You need a present for Aunt Rose Gardener and another one for little Jimmy Spacecadet and a third for your friend Monica Writer. But you've given Auntie Rose as many trowels and exotic tulip bulbs as she'll ever need, Jimmy has every cool toy his parents can buy him, and Monica treats *herself* to the hot new novels. What on earth should you choose for these dear people? Desperation is nipping at your heels.

You *have* come up with a lot of terrific gift ideas over the years, but you've forgotten a lot of them, too—and you just can't keep coming up with more. That's where *1,500 Great Gift Ideas* enters the picture. No more racking your brains, no more half-baked hunches, no more feeling like a heel when Cousin Susie Hopeful opens her present and her face falls at the sight of three more pairs of navy blue wool knee socks. From now on you'll have plenty of new

ideas and choices. Thumb through *1,500 Great Gift Ideas* to find the perfect present for Susie, Rose, Monica, or Jimmy—or Jimmy's mom, Jimmy's grandpa, or Jimmy's teacher. In this little book there's something wonderful for everyone, for every occasion, and in every price range.

For convenience, this book is divided into likely categories of gift giving, but don't be fenced in by categories. Browse through a variety of possibilities when you're looking for the right offering: For Dad you might want to check out "Deluxe Gifts," "Technogifts," and "Gifts for Readers and Writers." For Kathy Bestfriend, consider "Old-Fashioned Gifts" and "Really Great Clothing Gifts." Uncle Bob Trekker might like "Travel Gifts" or "Outdoorsy Gifts." Your niece, Liz Newlywed, could be a candidate for "Wedding Presents" or "Housewarming Presents." And for your sweetheart, try "Pampering Gifts" or "Traditional Gifts."

In addition to all this, the extras sprinkled throughout the book will enhance your gift-giving pleasure. You'll find advice on gift wrapping, catalog shopping, gift-buying strategies, presents for Valentine's Day, and more.

Some enthusiastic souls enjoy being completely consumed by the process of gift giving, but most of us don't have the time or energy for making a full-time career out of buying or creating presents. Happily, *1,500 Great Gift Ideas* takes you quickly and efficiently to the solutions you need, with as little decision-making anxiety as possible. Keep this book handy, and you'll never again be stumped by birthdays, anniversaries, or any other occasion. You'll find yourself being told—often—the words every gift giver *wants* to hear: "I love this! It's perfect!"

Traditional Gifts

Tradition can be a wonderful thing. This list includes some of the classics, the standards, *the* great gifts that are always welcome. Some of them are a bit pricey, it's true, but there *are* occasions when you want to throw caution to the winds and give the very best.

♦ TIP ♦

Think excellence, taste,
and long-lasting pleasure when
you give a traditional gift.

TRADITIONAL GIFTS

Leather wallet or billfold

Monogrammed money clip

Leather briefcase

Luggage—traditional leather is lovely, but you might like to go modern instead, and give a wheelie suitcase in microfiber or canvas.

Leather handbag or tote

Leather or suede gloves

Monogrammed silver flask

Fountain pen—gold- or silver-plated

Watch—gold, vintage, or bracelet

Dresser valet (for men)—this is usually made of fine wood, with drawers and compartments for coins, watch, keys, cell phone, glasses.

Jewelry box (for women)—leather or fabric, with trays, drawers, ring slots, etc.

Pearl necklace

Charm bracelet

Gold bangle bracelet

TRADITIONAL GIFTS

Cuff links (for men or women)

Cashmere scarf

Handkerchiefs—for men, choose fine cotton or linen, monogrammed or not; for women, fine cotton, batiste, or linen, with or without embroidery, monograms, or crochet or lace trim.

Leather or fur-lined bedroom slippers

Robe—for men, choose silk, terry cloth, flannel, seersucker, wool, or cashmere; for women, silk, satin, terry cloth, cotton or wool jersey, flannel, or cashmere. If you like, have the robe monogrammed.

Pajamas—broadcloth, silk, or flannel

TRADITIONAL GIFTS

Nightshirt—flannel, cotton, or silk

Bay rum cologne or aftershave

Silver-backed hairbrush

Tortoiseshell hairbrush and comb

Classic Panama hat

Silk tie

Damask or linen tablecloth and napkins

Napkin rings—silver, gold, or pewter,
with or without engraving

Rockingham teapot

Donation to a favorite cause

Old-Fashioned Gifts

These presents are not the latest fads or fashions—far from it, and thank heaven! Here's a list of tried-and-true gift ideas that have never lost their appeal. Some are a little nostalgic, some feel just as up-to-date today as they were decades ago, and all are solid favorites.

OLD-FASHIONED GIFTS

Little red wagon

Raggedy Ann and Andy dolls

Dollhouse

Chalkboard and colored chalk

Teddy bear

Marionette or puppet

Wooden blocks

Tinkertoys

Peanut brittle, maple sugar candy, fudge

Jams, jellies, and preserves

Penny candy—the Internet is chock-full of sources for *nostalgia candy,* and those are the key words to search for. You'll find old-fashioned penny candy, as well as candy from the 1950s and 1960s—Mary Janes, Sugar Daddies, red hots, jawbreakers, bubble-gum cigars, and more.

Pomander

Pillar candles scented with bayberry, pine, or cinnamon

Linen dish towels

Embroidered linen hand towels

Linen or damask tablecloth and matching napkins

Lace or crocheted tablecloth

Crocheted pot holders

Cast-iron skillet

Vintage kitchen utensils

Rockingham teapot

Cake stand

Pedestal stand with three tiers, for cookies, small cakes, meringues, etc., at tea time

Crystal punch bowl and cups

Earmuffs

OLD-FASHIONED GIFTS

Knitted mittens

Cashmere scarf and gloves

Cashmere ankle socks or knee socks

Slipper socks

Cotton pajamas

Flannel nightshirt or nightgown

Plaid wool or flannel robe

Flannel sheets

Hot-water bottle

Scented soap

OLD-FASHIONED GIFTS

Shaving brush and soap

Cameo

Pearl earrings or necklace

Tiepin or tie clasp

Pocket watch or classic wristwatch

Fountain pen

Leather wallet or change purse

Floral hankies for women, white cotton handkerchiefs for men

Oldies-but-goodies tape or CD

Patchwork quilt or pillow

OLD-FASHIONED GIFTS

Embroidered sampler or other folk art

Outfitted picnic basket, with plates, glasses, flatware, napkins, etc.

World atlas

Encyclopedia

Gift Wrapping

The important thing about gift wrapping is that you *do* it to each gift you give. It's the icing on the cake, the cherry on the sundae, the sprinkles on the ice cream cone. The wrapping doesn't have to be fancy, but it has to *be*—and it has to have ribbon (or something like ribbon) and a tag or card.

To this end, keep on hand a small stock of wrapping paper (rolls are best) in all-purpose patterns, such as stripes or dots, plus a few solid colors and a few specific-occasion papers, too (for birthdays, Christmas, and so on). Stash the papers in a big box, with a supply of curling and other ribbons, ready-made bows, simple tags or gift cards, tape, and scissors. Now you're ready for any wrapping challenge.

If you want to broaden your options, add these to your stash: large and small paper sacks in shiny or matte paper, with or without printed patterns; white and colored tissue paper; yarn to use in place of ribbon; metallic cord; stretch ties; pretty stickers and self-adhesive labels; glitter pens; colored markers.

◆ TIP ◆

Whenever you buy a gift, ask for a gift box. Everything looks better in a box, and it's a lot easier to wrap that way, too.

Gifts of Food

Whether homemade or store-bought, a gift of delicious food is always a treat, and there's something for everyone where food is concerned. Two minutes of thought (and a look at this list) will tell you what Marvin Goodeater or Amy Cookielover would like to get his or her teeth into. And if you can't quite decide on one single item, give a sampler of several goodies packed in a pretty basket, box, tote bag, or shiny paper shopping bag.

◆ TIP ◆

Keep in mind that the Internet is a great source of mail-order food gifts.

Gift baskets—buy these ready-made at a gourmet shop, specialty food store (such as a bakery or coffee-and-tea emporium), from a catalog, or from an on-line source. Your basket might feature a collection of: fruit, cookies, and chocolates; sausages and condiments; cheese and crackers; snacks; coffee and tea; regional specialties; jams and jellies.

Cookie collection in a pretty tin or other special packaging

GIFTS OF FOOD

Petit fours

Rugelach or coffee cake

Homemade pound cake

Homemade loaf cake—carrot, pumpkin, almond, lemon, etc.

Selection of hot-chocolate mixes

Chocolate-covered coffee beans

Imported chocolates

Assorted chocolates or a box of one special kind of candy, such as butter-crunch toffee, truffles, filled chocolates, or chocolate bark

Glacé chestnuts

Chocolate-dipped fruit or chocolate-covered nuts

Nostalgia candies—look for these in specialty candy stores, in catalogs, or on-line: Chuckles, Bit-O-Honey bars, Mary Janes, Sugar Daddies, Necco wafers, candy buttons, jawbreakers, root-beer barrels, bubble-gum cigars, licorice, and lots more.

Marzipan—classic fruit shapes, little animals, or with a holiday theme

Pistachios and other nuts—give lots!

Country ham

Selection of deli-style sausages and salamis

GIFTS OF FOOD

Smoked turkey

Smoked salmon

Caviar or salmon roe

Tin of pâté

Dried porcini mushrooms

Black or white truffle or truffle oil

Cheese straws

Selection of hard and soft cheeses

Vermont cheddar

Vermont maple syrup and maple sugar candy

Selection of barbecue sauces

Pickles and relishes, homemade or store-bought

Jars of orange marmalade, grapefruit marmalade, and lemon curd

Jars of honey—clover, thyme, buckwheat, orange blossom, etc.

Homemade soup

Homemade chili

Coffee Sampler: coffee beans, ground coffee, chocolate-covered coffee beans, measuring scoop

Tea Sampler: loose tea, teabags, strainer, tea ball, honey, tea biscuits

Italian Sampler: jars of olives, marinated artichokes, mushrooms, and roasted peppers; dry salami; wedge of Parmesan or Romano cheese; crusty bread or bread sticks; pasta; tomato paste; extra-virgin olive oil; balsamic vinegar; bulbs of garlic

Condiment Sampler: mild and hot chutney, hot sauce, two or three mustards, jar of capers, jars of olive paste and sun-dried tomato paste, salsa

Ice-cream Parlor Sampler: waffle or sugar cones, caramel or butterscotch sauce, bittersweet- or milk-chocolate sauce, fruit sauce, sprinkles, chopped nuts, candied cherries. If you like, include banana-split dishes or parfait glasses and an ice-cream scoop.

Breakfast Sampler: coffee beans (or ground coffee), smoked (nonperishable) bacon, granola, biscuit or muffin mix, buttermilk pancake mix, jam or marmalade, honey, maple syrup

Salad Sampler: extra-virgin olive oil, balsamic or red-wine vinegar, sea salt, croutons, powdered mustard, dried herbs, bulb of garlic. If you like, include salad tongs or salad-tossing fork and spoon.

PB & J Sampler: freshly made peanut butter (or other nut butter, if you prefer); fancy jellies such as apple, plum, quince, and currant

Gifts for Readers and Writers

If you know someone who loves to read (anything from magazines to romances to biographies) or loves to write (anything from thank-you notes to journals to novels), indulge him or her with one of the gifts from this list.

Book or books related to a favorite subject

Subscription to a book-of-the-month club—perhaps novels, mysteries, or a special subject, such as crafts or history

Dictionary

Thesaurus

Reference book, such as a book of quotations, a single-volume encyclopedia, an almanac, etc.

Personalized book plates

Subscription to a literary magazine or a magazine for writers

Battery-operated reading lamp that attaches to a book, for reading at night

Small or large magnifying lens, for reading the small print. Look for a small lens on a chain that can be worn around the neck, a pocket-style lens, or perhaps a large lens with built-in light.

Surprise!

Instead of simply handing over your gift, add some drama and a lot of fun by turning the occasion into a surprise for him or her:

- ◆ Hide the gift in the fridge, then ask her to get you a glass of milk.

- ◆ Drop the gift at his mom's house, then beg him to go over and pick up the package you *accidentally* left over there.

- ◆ Wrap a small gift in a huge box.

- ◆ Bury a small gift in a big tin of pistachios, pretzels, or popcorn.

- ◆ Hide a few gifts all over the house, then send her on a scavenger hunt.

- Stash the gift in the attic (or cellar), then develop a burning need for something stored up (or down) there—something only he can find for you.

- Put the gift in the bathtub, behind the shower curtain. (Don't let her turn on the water!)

- Hide the gift in his underwear drawer.

- Mail it to him at work.

- Take her out for dinner and have the waiter present the gift.

Tilt-top bed desk, for reading or writing in bed

Portable desk—this wonderful contraption sits on the lap and usually has pockets or compartments for stationery, envelopes, pens, stamps, postcards, and so on.

Desk accessories—choose any or all of these: desk pad, letter box, business-card holder, notepad holder, pen cup, picture frame, letter opener, stacking desk trays.

Writer's supplies—printer paper, pens, markers, red pencils, stick-on notes, etc.

Personalized notepads

Small cassette or digital recorder for making verbal notes

Notebook (or laptop) computer light that plugs into a port and lights keyboard or notes

Stationery of all kinds—plain, personalized, business, foldover cards, matching envelopes, etc.

Box of pretty note cards

Selection of postcards (plain, personalized, or with pictures) and an equal number of stamps

Fountain pen or any other jazzy pen, such as a sleek ballpoint pen on a chain to wear around the neck

Colored inks (in bottles or cartridges) for use with a fountain pen

Calligraphy pens and ink, plus appropriate paper or note cards

Calligraphy markers in several colors, plus appropriate paper or note cards

Night writer—this is a gadget has a built-in light and holds a pad and pen for jotting down middle-of-the-night thoughts or dreams.

Antique typewriter

Gifts for Looking and Feeling Attractive

How we look often influences how we feel—and when we feel good, we usually look good. Helping someone feel or look good is a pretty nice thing to do, and here's a no-fail list of possibilities for the men and women in your life. (And give yourself a little present while you're at it. You deserve it.)

GIFTS FOR LOOKING AND FEELING ATTRACTIVE

Gift certificate for manicure and/or pedicure, including hand or foot massage

Battery-operated manicure and pedicure set, with attachments

Set of nail tools, including cuticle scissors, cuticle nipper, nail clippers, etc.

Selection of nail- and hand-care products: emery boards, cuticle remover, repair kit, buffer, nail polish, topcoat, polish remover, nail strengthener, hand cream, gel or moisturizing gloves

Selection of foot-care products: soothing foot soak, pumice stone, foot smoother with coarse and fine surfaces, softening cream (and a pair of cotton socks), gel or moisturizing socks

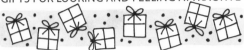

Waxing kit

Electric shaver for a man or woman—
buy the best you can afford.

Selection of shaving products for men:
shaving soap and brush, preshave oil or
lotion, shaving cream or gel, shower
shaving lotion, aftershave cream or
lotion, astringent, moisturizer

Selection of bath and body products:
bath salts, pearls, or tablets; bubble
bath; cleanser; moisturizer; bath and
shower gel; soap

Long-handled bath brush, loofah, and
natural sponge

Selection of skin-care products: face-cleansing lotion, mask, body lotion, toner, exfoliating wash, moisturizer for day or night, sunscreen, eye treatment

Selection of hair-care products: shampoo, conditioner, styling spray, styling gel or cream, antifrizz, glossing cream, mousse, sun protectant

Salon-quality hair dryer or blow dryer

Hot rollers or hot comb

Fine hairbrush

Travel brush and comb

Hair-care-products travel kit

Gift certificate for beauty products

Selection of lip products: lipstick, lip pencil, liquid lipstick, lip gloss, palette of lip colors, lip balm, lip plumper

Selection of eye products: individual eye shadow, palette of eye shadows, eyeliner, eye pencils, mascara, eyelash curler, eyebrow color, eye cream, concealer

Makeup brush set

Makeup mirror with lights

Aromatherapy kit

Fragrance for women: perfume, cologne, collection of products in the same fragrance, purse spray, travel kit (spray cologne, body lotion, bath gel, etc.), soap

Fragrance for men: cologne, shaving kit (cleanser, shaving cream, aftershave), travel kit (shampoo, cleanser, body lotion, etc.), soap

Shoeshine kit

Really Great Clothing Gifts

Children are all too well known for hating gifts of clothing, but that's not the case with 99 percent of grown-ups and teenagers! Something new to wear is *exciting* and always welcome—unless you make the mistake of giving Niece Janie Hipteen a droopy mauve cardigan or Second Cousin Martha Straitlace an itsy-bitsy stretch camisole.

◆ TIP ◆

Give a major-investment garment (such as a winter coat) only when you know the person's taste very well—or buy from a local store that doesn't mind returns or exchanges. Ditto for tricky-to-fit things like pants and serious shoes. When in doubt, a gift certificate is the way to go.

REALLY GREAT CLOTHING GIFTS

Sweater in the very latest style or material—ask at the store if you're not sure what's hot

Classic cashmere crewneck, V-neck, or turtleneck sweater

Cotton "cashmere" sweater

Cotton or cashmere twin set

Big, soft pullover sweater—think cozy, sit-by-the-fire, after-ski, or homebound-in-a-blizzard, and choose bouclé, fleece, polyester-and-cotton, velour, French terry, acrylic-and-wool, chenille, or any other comfy material.

Silk jersey sweater

Silk T-shirt

Stack of great short-sleeved T-shirts—giving several T-shirts makes it a special present. Check the Internet for mail-order sources.

Long-sleeved T-shirt in a solid color or stripes

Classic turtleneck in a great color

Latest style of turtleneck, perhaps a funnel neck or mock neck

Jersey top in a great color or stripe—look for interesting sleeves (cap, elbow-length, ribbed) and a great neckline (V-neck, scoop, keyhole, collared, slashed, boat).

REALLY GREAT CLOTHING GIFTS

Classic polo or rugby shirt

Classic French sailor jersey with blue-
and-white stripes

Regular tank top in cotton, silk, cashmere,
wool, or stretch fabric

Skimpy tank top, perhaps with spaghetti
straps or straps that cross in back

Camisole to wear as a layering piece,
in stretchy or lacy fabric

Egyptian cotton shirt

Crisp white shirt or blouse in cotton or
a cotton blend, with nice detailing

Button-down oxford-cloth shirt

Broadcloth or other cotton shirt in stripes, checks, plaid, or other simple pattern

Aloha shirt, vintage shirt, or shirt with a wild pattern

Linen or silk shirt

Suede shirt

Suede or leather skirt

Suede or leather pants or jeans

Suede jacket or blazer

Leather jacket—choose lined or unlined, and look for a great new style. Bomber jackets are terrific for guys.

REALLY GREAT CLOTHING GIFTS

Rain jacket or slicker—pick something fun and waterproof, possibly with a hood, possibly in a bright color like lime, fuchsia, turquoise, fire engine red, or orange.

Light windbreaker

French terry zip-up jacket with hood

Silk sport jacket

Linen blazer

Wool flannel blazer

Cashmere-blend blazer

Jean jacket

Cool jeans, cords, or chinos

REALLY GREAT CLOTHING GIFTS

Linen slacks, capris, or shorts

Dressy slacks

Dressy skirt (short or long) in velvet, satin, silk, crepe, synthetic, or other fabric

Party dress

Elegantly tailored suit

Vest for man or woman—silk, down, embroidered, fake fur, quilted, patch-work, or other material

Wrinkle-resistant separates for travel

Anything sparkly or glittery, for holiday wear

Wrapping a Gift of Food

Presentation is important when you're giving a gift of food because the visual message signals the go-ahead to the taste buds. Whether the gift is homemade or store-bought, the wrapping should be appetizing, and it should also protect the food from breakage and contamination. Here are some suggestions for attractive containers and gift wraps:

- Cookies: Pile carefully in a pretty bowl, straw basket, plastic berry basket, small white painter's bucket, or child's plastic bucket that you've lined with bright tissue paper or cellophane. Tie with ribbon.

- Loaf cakes, fruitcakes, breads: Wrap snugly in cellophane or plastic wrap. Place on a wooden breadboard, pretty tray, serving platter, or in a baking tin. Add a ribbon bow.

- Candy, nuts, snack mixtures: Pack into a big jar, white cardboard take-out food container, cloth drawstring bag, or shiny paper sack. Add a bow and label.

- Other possible containers: cookie jar, cookie tin, mushroom basket, child's lunch box, coffee tin, plastic or clay flowerpot, shiny paper shopping bag

Really Great Accessories

All dressed up and—no jazzy handbag? No perfect earrings? No fabulous tie? No cool shoes? No wardrobe could possibly contain too many accessories, so this category will accommodate a slew of gift-giving occasions. When you're picking an accessory, think about the lifestyle, taste, and age of the recipient; it's probably best not to give Mildred Tailormade an ankle bracelet or Kimberly Discodancer a classic leather handbag she wouldn't be caught dead with. On the other hand, an accessory that's a bit daring or unusual could start a whole new fashion adventure for Beverly Plainjane. You never know.

Chic sunglasses

Belt in fine leather, suede, webbing, ribbon, etc.—look for interesting details, such as rings, buckles, fringe, etc.

Silk tie

Fancy suspenders

Evening bag—beaded, embroidered, satin, velvet, etc.

Straw bag for summer

Tiny handbag or shoulder bag with pockets, just big enough for cards, money, lipstick, and a pen

Canvas-and-leather handbag

Classic leather handbag

Fun leather handbag—check the latest style and go for it!

"Healthy back" bag or backpack

Tote bag in leather, linen, cotton, woven plastic, waterproof rubber, etc.

Weekender bag in leather, canvas, microfiber, etc. Look for interesting features such as leather handles, pockets, or zippered compartments.

Leather or microfiber zip-up wallet

Dressy scarf to wear at the neck—silk, chiffon, satin, or velvet

Outdoor scarf—cashmere, wool, angora, mohair, chenille, velvet, etc. (Add a matching hat or gloves for a larger present.)

Leather or suede gloves, either unlined or lined with silk or wool. Look for interesting details, such as fur trim, fringe, buckles, contrast stitching, or contrast welting.

Dressy gloves, perhaps satin or super-soft leather

Earrings—so many styles to choose from: contemporary, classic, vintage, Victorian, sparkly, feathered, large, small, tailored, dangly, and so on.

Ankle bracelet

REALLY GREAT ACCESSORIES

Charm bracelet, with meaningful charms or just plain fun charms

Pizzazzy watch—inexpensive or expensive, in the latest hip style

Necklace or bracelet with semiprecious stones, such as amethyst, garnet, aquamarine, topaz, turquoise; with freshwater pearls; with amber, coral, agate, or crystal

Jewelry featuring the birthstone of the giftee

Vintage jewelry—for example, plastic from the 1930s and 1940s, costume jewelry from the 1950s, or jet and marcasite from the early twentieth century

REALLY GREAT ACCESSORIES

Leather or suede jewelry

Clogs with uppers in wool, leather, fleece, or suede

Hottest new walking or running shoes

Gift certificate for shoes or boots from a good store

Several pairs of special socks—trouser socks, argyles, embroidered, etc.

Panty hose or tights—sheers, fun colors or patterns, fishnet, and so on

Regular or folding umbrella—how about giving three inexpensive folding umbrellas to the person who's always losing his umbrella at work or leaving hers in a taxicab?

Flip-flops in a cool color

Rain boots, possibly in bright yellow, red, or basic black

Fun straw hat for the beach

Cowboy hat

Baseball cap

Winter hat in fake fur, leather, suede, fleece, cashmere

Knitted or crocheted cap—look for fun yarns (cotton, nubby silk, chenille, variegated colors) and details such as pompoms, contrasting cuff, worked-in pattern, or ribbing.

Earmuffs in fur, fake fur, or fleece

Hair accessories: ornaments, combs, pins, clips, barrettes, scrunchies, headbands, flowers, or fasteners for twists and other updos

Big shawl in soft wool, fleece, velour, chenille, cashmere, or cut velvet

Knitted or crocheted shawl

Filmy stole for evening wear

Pampering Gifts

Pampering is something that most of us need more of, so encourage your partner, friend, or relative to indulge him- or herself—by offering any of the delightful gifts listed here. And remember: Pampering can be as simple as taking a bubble bath or as luxurious as delving into an ounce of caviar. Whatever works.

PAMPERING GIFTS

Gift certificate for a full-body massage—or more than one massage!

Gift certificate for a back or neck rub

Personal massager

Massage oil

Trip to a weeklong yoga retreat or a week at a spa

Spa-treats Sampler: body lotion, massage oil, facial mask, gel gloves, gel socks, and more

Gift certificate for spa services, including massage, body wrap, facial, manicure, pedicure

PAMPERING GIFTS

His-and-hers all-day session at a day spa

Aromatherapy kit

Aromatherapy accessories: booties, gloves, eye pillow with herbal fills, etc.

Sachets

Fragrance: perfume, cologne, candles, etc.

Potpourri

Floral bath powder

Selection of soaps—this gift might include perfumed soaps (floral, herbal, spicy), soaps in bright colors or fun shapes, and healing or curative soaps.

PAMPERING GIFTS

Bath salts or bubble bath

Bath-Treats Sampler: bath oil, soaps, fizzy bath tablets, soft washcloth, candle

Super-soft Egyptian cotton washcloths

Oversized bath towel

Terry shower wrap

Back scrubber, body scrubber

Handheld showerhead

Waterproof shower radio

Fabulous hairbrush

Satin nightgown and robe

Soft wool bed jacket

Silk pajamas

Silk kimono

Satin slippers, perhaps trimmed with marabou

Silk or chiffon shawl

Lacy teddy or camisole

Five pairs of sheer, silky panty hose

Presents Plus

When is a present not a present? When it's two presents—one (or more!) tucked inside the other. Here are some great combinations:

- ◆ Beautiful evening bag packed with a little mad money, new lipstick, silk scarf, pretty change purse, or sparkly earrings

- ◆ Leather handbag containing fountain pen, memo pad and pencil, eyeglass case, or cell phone

- ◆ Small backpack holding a disposable camera, walk-around radio, pedometer, water bottle, or packets of trail mix

- ◆ Clay or ceramic plant pot stuffed with gardening gloves, seed packets, bulbs, or trowel

- ◆ Child's overnight case chock-full of small games, puzzles, or toys

- Bookbag packed with paperback dictionary and thesaurus, school supplies, fancy mouse pad, colored pencils, spiral notepads, or Magic Markers
- Cosmetics carryall filled with skin-care goodies, hair clips and barrettes, eye makeup, packets of bubble bath, or nail polish
- Small travel case loaded with travel-size shampoo, soap, toothpaste, moisturizer, shower cap, first-aid kit, mending kit
- Canvas shoulder bag holding baby care products, infant toys, baby socks, or tiny T-shirts
- Lacy lingerie case stuffed with pairs of panty hose, perfume, sachets, silk bikinis, or ankle bracelet
- CD carrier holding a couple of CDs, concert tickets, or gift certificate for a music store

PAMPERING GIFTS

Feather boa

Custom-made shoes, handbag, or suit

Warm winter boots

Padded satin hangers

Luxurious sheets and pillowcases

Electric bed warmer

Feather pillow

Herbal therapy pillow

Featherbed

Down comforter

Really good bedside reading lamp

PAMPERING GIFTS

Selection of herbal teas

Chocolate truffles

Frosted cupcakes

Petit fours

Jar of macadamia nuts

Caviar

Lobster dinner

Dinner without the kids

Corsage of violets

Fresh flowers every week for a dozen weeks

PAMPERING GIFTS

Session with a professional makeup artist

Session with a personal trainer

New air conditioner

Water pitcher with filter

One month of car service to the office

Second phone line

Gifts That
Give Comfort

Comfort comes in many forms. It might be something to wear, to eat, or to soothe the body or soul. It's usually something that makes life a little easier, offers support, or feels very healing in the face of physical or emotional pain. Don't wait for a special occasion to give a comforting gift—give it whenever you see it's needed.

Homemade chicken soup

Favorite candy, whatever it might be—
find out!

Homemade or bakery cookies—old
familiars such as chocolate chip, oatmeal,
sugar, or butter cookies, as well as
shortbread or gingersnaps

GIFTS THAT GIVE COMFORT

Old-fashioned baked goods, such as banana bread, gingerbread, pecan pie, apple pie, cinnamon rolls, biscuits, brownies, popovers, muffins—you get the idea

Tea for one—either a nested set of cup and small teapot, or a small teapot and a pretty mug, plus loose tea or teabags

Coffee for one—one-cup drip filter, filter papers, delicious ground coffee, and a mug

Commuter's mug

Lumbar pillow

Adjustable wristbands

Gel socks and/or gloves

Small soft blanket for office, car, train, plane

Soft sweatpants and sweatshirt

Soft afghan in lamb's wool, cashmere, chenille, mohair

Soft shawl in mohair, cashmere, fleece, wool blend

Soft robe in chenille, cashmere, cotton jersey, French terry

Bed jacket in chenille, silk, satin, warm wool

Soft cotton or silk pajamas or nightgown

GIFTS THAT GIVE COMFORT

Moisture-wicking pajamas or nightgown

Soft cotton jersey sleep shirt

Fuzzy fleece bedroom slippers

Slipper socks

Fleece socks

Bed lounging pillow, for reading, watching TV, etc.

Fleece lounging sack—a big roomy "sack" that zips up the front, with cuffs at the ankle

Sleep mask

New bed or mattress

Feather bed or thick fleece mattress pad, for a heavenly night's sleep

Feather pillow

Down comforter

Nighttime sleep-inducing sound generator—look for one that offers a choice of sounds so the giftee can pick the one that works best for him or her.

Electric blanket

Hot-water bottle with flannel or fleece jacket

Deluxe heating pad

GIFTS THAT GIVE COMFORT

Cold pack—look for the newest technology

Bed tray with folding legs

Humidifier or combination humidifier and air cleaner

Air purifier

Full-spectrum lamp

Jet spa for the tub—cordless, of course

Foot spa, with water jets, massaging rollers, other attachments

Towel warming rack

Evening out after a hard week

Afternoon with a personal shopper—you! Take a friend shopping, help her find and purchase everything on her list, and finish up with a nice dinner to celebrate.

Day off alone, to do anything or nothing

Day off together—to have fun, rekindle romance, get away from the daily grind

Friendship photo album—start this album for a friend, using pictures you've taken, and leave blank pages for her to fill, too.

Remembrance of someone who has passed away—this may sound like a strange gift, but it is not. Great comfort can be taken from holding and touching something a loved one has owned and enjoyed—a small object, a book, a journal, a chess set, a bracelet. A framed photo makes a wonderful remembrance, too.

Valentine's Day Gifts

On February 14, love is in the air—and presents are tucked under the arm, for delivery with a kiss. Here are some sweet and loving possibilities:

- Heart-shaped box of chocolates—sure, it's old hat, but who doesn't love getting chocolates?
- Roses, of course—fresh or silk
- Heart-shaped jewelry—perhaps a pendant set with diamonds, or a red enamel pin
- Any piece of jewelry nestled in a heart-shaped box
- Weekend at a romantic inn
- Trip to the Tunnel of Love
- Fabulous dinner at the most romantic restaurant in town
- Breakfast in bed—with heart-shaped pancakes

- Red gloves—fine leather or suede would be nice
- Red shoes
- Red cashmere sweater
- Lingerie—red! And what about boxer shorts printed with hearts?
- Satin nightgown or pajamas
- Romantic (or sexy) board, dice, or card game
- Stuffed animal bearing a small gift—gold locket, ring, a few perfect chocolate truffles
- Perfume—be sure to get a scent she likes
- ID bracelet engraved with both your names
- Jar full of love notes written on slips of paper
- Love poems—a book of them or one of your very own
- Music box with "your" song on it
- Matching rings

Deluxe Gifts

Deluxe means different things to different people. If you're very, very rich, deluxe might mean a brand-new oceangoing yacht or his-and-hers Porsches. If you're a struggling grad student, deluxe might mean a steak dinner. In this list you'll find a wide range of deluxe possibilities to choose from.

DELUXE GIFTS

Dinner at a four-star restaurant

Dinner at a favorite restaurant

Champagne and champagne flutes

Case of wine

Ounce or two of caviar

Microwave oven

Washer and dryer

Television

Handheld color television

Plug-in color TV for car

Portable DVD player

Mobile movie theater for car, boat, summer house

Complete home audio system

CD stereo

Cell phone, plus a year of service

Lounge chair

Freestanding hammock

Ergonomically correct desk chair

Furniture—anything from a rolltop desk to a leather sofa, Chinese chairs to marble end tables

Home gym equipment

DELUXE GIFTS

Racing bike—the best!

Pitching or batting machine

Pool table and accessories

Leather golf bag

Golf-bag caddy (on wheels)

Leather-boxed poker set

Telescope

Motorized scooter

Backyard play equipment, such as swings, seesaw, sandbox

Backyard playhouse

DELUXE GIFTS

Oversized stuffed animal

Baby's engraved silver mug, cup, or spoon

Cashmere baby clothes

Cashmere sweater or shawl

Elbow-length evening gloves

Custom-made suit

Custom-made shoes

Electric shoe polisher

Leather jewelry box, with suede lining, removable tray, pockets, compartments, lock and key

DELUXE GIFTS

Diamonds or pearls—earrings, bracelet, necklace, ring

Cashmere throw or blanket

Fine cotton sheets and pillowcases, perhaps trimmed with lace, embroidery, or eyelet

King-size down comforter

Personalized embosser and heavy, elegant stationery on which to use it

First-edition book or other rare volume—choose a favorite novel or children's book, a book about a favorite topic, or perhaps a book of poetry.

Coffee-table book of fine reproductions of paintings

Original art—painting, drawing, sculpture, print (etching, lithograph, silkscreen, etc.)

Art glass or art pottery

Antique—this might be a piece of furniture, fine mirror, lamp, tapestry, quilt, china, silver- or gold-plated object, pewter object, vintage toy, memorabilia, collectible, vintage phonograph and cylinders, or snow globe.

Day trip on a yacht or sailboat

Trip or vacation to an exotic place

DELUXE GIFTS

Trip to a dream—this trip is for satisfying a passion for a particular person, place, thing, event, or subject matter. Your giftee might dream of going to Graceland, the Alamo, the Rock and Roll Hall of Fame, the Baseball Hall of Fame, Gettysburg, Hollywood, Colonial Williamsburg, or Monticello. These are all in the U.S.A., of course, but remember that the entire world is available!

Inexpensive Gifts

You don't have to spend a bundle on every gift—you really don't. There are lots of sweet, fun, thoughtful, delightful presents to choose from here (and in other sections, too).

◆ TIP ◆

If your city has street vendors, you can often pick up great bargains at their tables. Depending on the season, buy hats and gloves, sunglasses, fun fad jewelry, fun socks, scarves, handbags, books, games, toys.

Flowering plant

Two or three small pots of herbs—
oregano, chives, basil, rosemary, thyme,
tarragon, sage

Something delicious to eat—give a single
yummy item: good olive oil; real maple
syrup; tin of shortbread; biscotti; jar of
marmalade, lemon curd, or fruit butter;
big bag of pistachios; licorice all-sorts;
fudge; jelly beans; big bar of chocolate;
candied ginger, and so on.

INEXPENSIVE GIFTS

Kitchen gadgets—peeler, whisk, pizza cutter, measuring spoons, etc.

Pretty chopsticks—plastic or wood, in bright colors, patterned or inlaid

Set of six French jelly-glass tumblers with lids

Set of inexpensive wineglasses or champagne flutes

Votive candles and holders

Set of coasters

Fridge magnets

Party supplies, such as paper napkins, guest towels, paper plates, in bright colors

INEXPENSIVE GIFTS

Paperback books—choose three or four new novels, all (or several of) the books by a favorite author, several books on one topic (such as knitting, the Civil War, antiques, food), or children's titles.

Eyeglass case

Leather coin purse

Zipper cases for cosmetics, handbag, travel, school, etc.

Videotape or DVD of a favorite movie

Handheld cassette recorder and microcassettes

Calculator

INEXPENSIVE GIFTS

Playing cards

Dartboard and darts

Sports jump rope with covered wood handles and ball bearings

Toys—yo-yo, pickup sticks, marbles, jacks, jump rope, Slinky

Bicycle bell

Coloring books

Set of fun markers—glitter, gel, bright colors, neon, etc.

Postcards—pick a theme or just choose a stack of pretty or interesting ones.

INEXPENSIVE GIFTS

Note cards

Calendar for wall or desk

Hair accessories—comb, scrunchy,
ponytail holder, beads, flowers, clips,
headband

Earmuffs

Wool or angora gloves

Fun socks

The Gift That Keeps On Giving

These wonderful gifts are repeaters. They either: a) arrive every day or week; b) arrive three, six, nine, or twelve times a year; c) are used at regular intervals; d) are used several times, at the discretion of the recipient; or e) are received once, but have an impact that lasts and lasts.

THE GIFT THAT KEEPS ON GIVING

Gift-of-the-month-club subscription—
these gift clubs will deliver goodies
three, six, nine, or twelve times during
the year. Choose from flowers, plants,
fruit, entrées, wine, beer, pasta, pizza,
salsa, pie, cake, cheesecake, cookies,
jelly, tea, coffee, chocolate, and more.
Simply order from a catalog or find them
on the Internet by doing a search for
"fruit-of-the-month," "wine-of-the-month,"
and so on.

Gift-basket-of-the-month-club subscription—similar to a gift-of-the-month club,
a gift-basket-of-the-month club delivers
a variety of food and other items each
month.

Magazine subscription—think about giving a subscription to a magazine that features news, fashion, a special field of interest (such as fishing, knitting, or yoga), puzzles, food, sports, etc. There's a magazine for everyone. Children's magazines are great gifts for kids, too.

Newspaper subscription—a local newspaper is always a good gift, but consider a subscription to a foreign-language newspaper, a paper from another city, or a financial paper.

Cable, satellite, or pay-per-view TV for one, six, or twelve months

Membership to a local public radio or TV station

THE GIFT THAT KEEPS ON GIVING

Membership to a local museum or arts center

Subscription to a theater, ballet, opera, or concert series

Donation in the name of the recipient—making a donation to someone's favorite charity, school, or cause is a gift that keeps on giving in a different way. Here are some places to which you might consider making a donation:

- Hospital or hospice
- University, local college, special school
- Community center or settlement house
- Organization doing research on a specific disease

THE GIFT THAT KEEPS ON GIVING

- ◆ Homeless shelter
- ◆ Church group
- ◆ Animal-related organization (pet adoption agency, shelter, rescue mission)
- ◆ Soup kitchen, food bank, or group taking food to the elderly or shut-ins
- ◆ Children's charities and aid societies
- ◆ Funds for police and firefighters
- ◆ Umbrella organizations (large charities that fund many kinds of programs)

Homemade coupons for services you can perform—coupons should be tailored to the needs of the giftee and are to be used as needed. Give coupons for:

- ◆ Baby-sitting
- ◆ Ironing or laundry

THE GIFT THAT KEEPS ON GIVING

- ◆ Making breakfast or any other meal
- ◆ Acting as a "personal shopper"
- ◆ Mending or sewing
- ◆ Home or car repair
- ◆ Performing a morning or afternoon of chores
- ◆ Yard or garden work
- ◆ Companionship time—time spent together
- ◆ Talk time—time spent listening or problem solving
- ◆ Fun time—time spent playing Scrabble, dancing, picnicking, or doing whatever your giftee chooses

Seasonal Gifts

All four seasons offer inventive gift-giving possibilities, but winter—who can deny it?—is wide open for holiday-related presents.

◆ TIP ◆

You don't necessarily have to give a seasonal gift during its obvious season. Seasonal gifts can *anticipate* the coming season. Give Christmas ornaments in autumn, tulip bulbs in winter, a beach tote in spring, or a shiny new leaf rake in summer. When the appropriate season arrives and the gift is put to use— you're a hero!

Winter

Calendar for the new year

Logs for the fireplace—give them in a handsome carrier or just haul them to the shed and stack them up—then bring your giftee out to see her bounty.

Fireplace supplies: long matches in a holder, andirons, tools (broom, shovel, hook, tongs, poker), basket or other container for storing logs, fireplace gloves, nylon or canvas log carrier, hearth rug, fire screen, potpourri for fire

Christmas gift basket of food treats

Gingerbread house

SEASONAL GIFTS

CD or tape of Christmas carols or Handel's *Messiah*

Homemade CD of holiday or seasonal songs

Video or DVD of Christmas movie

Christmas wreath, with or without trimmings

Pillar candles scented with bayberry or spice

Ornaments for the tree

SEASONAL GIFTS

Top-of the-tree ornament

Christmas tree skirt

Christmas craft kits: crewel, cross-stitch, embroidery, felt, ornaments, wreath, gingerbread house

Christmas place mats

Personalized Christmas stockings

Christmas tablecloth and napkins

Advent calendar

Poinsettia plant

Christmas cactus

Amaryllis or other bulb

SEASONAL GIFTS

Christmas or Hanukkah cookie collection

Menorah

Set of dreidels

Hanukkah candles

Hanukkah music or video

Spring

Flower bulbs

Flowering plant

Easter lily or other potted plant

Strawberry preserves made with whole fruit

Anything with a strawberry theme—
bowls, plates, jam jar, dish towels,
napkins, etc.

Asparagus steamer

Serving dish for asparagus

Summer

Fitted picnic basket

Tall tumblers (for lemonade or iced tea)

Iced-tea spoons

Hibachi

Coal or gas grill

SEASONAL GIFTS

Barbecue accessories—fork, tongs, mitts, etc.

Beach tote

Beach chairs

Beach umbrella

Inflatable for beach or pool

Wind chimes or whirligig

Fall

Chrysanthemum plant or other autumn flowering plant

Carved pumpkin

Grapevine wreath—trim with bittersweet, lady apples, autumn leaves,
ribbon bows, or any other decoration,
if you like.

Leaf-grabber rake

Birdbath or bird feeder

Welcome mat in fall colors

Copper wash boiler or copper bucket.
Copper is a beautiful color for fall. Fill
the boiler or bucket with branches of
autumn leaves, firethorn, or bittersweet
for a perfect October gift.

Graduation Gifts

Graduations are marker events and deserve to be celebrated with gifts. For any graduation, from middle school to graduate school, money is always an appropriate gift. So, indeed, is the traditional watch. But if you want to get a little more personal, choose from the list that follows.

High School Graduation

If the graduate is finished with school and starting a job, any gift from a new suit to a new car is great. If the graduate is going to continue living at home, give him something for his living space. If the graduate is moving out to a new apartment, see the list under College Graduation, page 112.

For high school graduate staying at home:

TV for bedroom

Six months of premium-cable channel

Phone line of his own

GRADUATION GIFTS

Portable phone

Cell phone

Beeper

Telephone answering machine

Redecoration of bedroom

Long-term subway, bus, or train fare
card or commuter pass

**For high school graduate going
away to college:**

Luggage—wheelie, duffel bag, soft
suitcase

New clothes

GRADUATION GIFTS

Notebook (or laptop) computer

Notebook (or laptop) carrying case—
simple style or style with pockets for
disks, mouse, etc., in leather, canvas,
suede, microfiber

CD player

Small TV for college dormitory room

Clock radio

Clock radio–CD player combo

Dictionary and thesaurus

Class and study supplies: notebooks,
pens, paper, note cards, battery-
powered pencil sharpener, clips, tape,
Zip disks, etc.

Carryall briefcase for books, with pockets for smaller things like pens, note cards, etc.

Heavy-duty backpack with all the bells and whistles—water bottle, organizing pockets, etc.

Rolling bookpack—this is essentially a backpack with wheels, for carrying heavy books, schoolwork, etc.— especially useful on a large campus.

Cell phone

Phone card

College Graduation

Tickets for a trip

Luggage for a trip

Gift that goes with new career—depending on the career, you might give a briefcase, PDA, notebook (or laptop) computer, leather-bound date-book, portfolio, uniform, good walking shoes, business suit, etc.

GRADUATION GIFTS

Basic supplies for new apartment—this might be kitchen equipment, dishes, flatware, sheets, towels, set of spices, a case of canned soup, blankets, down quilt, comforter, bedspread, bed, pillows, desk, lamps, futon, and so on.

Cell phone

Phone card

Beeper

Mother's Day and Father's Day Gifts

In most families, Mother's Day and Father's Day are important holidays and not to be taken lightly. The matter of a gift looms large, but that shouldn't scare you. These are occasions on which you simply want to make Mom or Dad smile, smile, smile and feel totally appreciated. That's the whole—the *only*—goal. Let them know how much you honor, respect, enjoy, and treasure them.

For starters, neither Mother's Day nor Father's Day may be the right day for a strictly practical gift—unless your parent is a strictly practical sort of person. And that's the key to success: knowing who your mom or dad really is. Is she a perfume-and-earrings type? Is he a barbecue-and-softball sort? What frivolous or useful item has she been mentioning lately? What playful or down-to-earth thing has he been pointing out recently? If you don't know, it's your job to try to find out ASAP.

If the clues are few, don't despair. Look through all the sections of this book that seem to apply to your particular parent—perhaps "Gifts for the Cook" (page 217), "Technogifts" (page 273), "Outdoorsy Gifts" (page 247), or "Gifts That Give Comfort" (page 67). Let your heart lead you, and you'll know the perfect gift the moment you see it.

Engagement-Shower Gifts

An engagement-shower (or prewedding-party) gift is usually more modest than a wedding gift, which leaves plenty of room for variety and invention. If the couple is registered, of course you can give them something from their list—that's a surefire winner. If they're not registered, you might want to give them something that pertains to their mutual special interests—perhaps a) opera, b) camping, c) antiques, d) ice hockey, or e) Chihuahuas, which might yield: a) CDs of their favorite opera or opera singer, b) a new camp stove, c) a small antique mirror, d) tickets to the next game, or e) a photo album for doggy pix.

If the shower has a theme, you're on easy street: Either the hosts will give you a pretty clear idea of what to bring, or you'll just fall in with the theme. Here are a few more ways to handle the shower gift:

- Kick in with a few of your buddies so you can buy a somewhat larger present.

- You (or you and a friend) can put together a basketful of little gifts. Choose beauty products, kitchen gadgets, bath products, games and puzzles, garden items (including bulbs and seeds), or travel-size stuff for the honeymoon trip.

ENGAGEMENT-SHOWER GIFTS

- Give them *lots* of just one thing—
  a one-year supply of, for instance,
  disposable cameras, paper towels,
  coffee filters, taco chips, cat food,
  pistachio nuts, light bulbs, Ziploc bags,
  chocolate bars, or stick-on notes.

- Give the gift of time and effort:
  Shower guests might meet at the
  couple's new home to clean, paint,
  repair, or simply help unpack the
  moving cartons.

- Celebrate two: Give two champagne
  flutes and a bottle of bubbly; a pair of
  soft terry shower wraps; two down
  pillows; two mugs, personalized; a
  couple of favorite movies on DVD or
  video; two tickets to hear the singer
  or group they love most; a two-year
  subscription to their favorite magazine
  or newspaper.

◆ If she's taking her groom's surname,
give her something monogrammed
with her new initials: gold ankle
bracelet, cuff links, crisp white shirt,
turtleneck, terry robe, canvas tote
bag, or baseball cap. Or have something printed with her new name:
informal stationery, folded note
cards, business cards, or memo pads.

Oh, and don't forget a touch of trash
along with all the fun—what's an
engagement shower without those two
or three silly but *très risqué* items?

Lingerie—bikini panties, lacy camisole, nightgown, robe, baby-doll pj's, fancy panty hose or stockings

Jewelry—pick fun things, such as sparkly earrings, bangle bracelets, colorful costume jewelry, a pin that reflects one of her special interests (music, flowers, cooking), a glittery necklace, something with her birthstone in it, or a pretty watch.

ENGAGEMENT-SHOWER GIFTS

Brunch for two at their favorite
restaurant

CDs of romantic songs

Two dozen candles in a rainbow of colors

Picture frame or photo album

Wedding journal

Travel guide to the honeymoon spot

Wedding Presents

These are usually more substantial than engagement gifts and are often chosen from the couple's registry. Using the registry cuts down on mistakes, but you don't have to use it if you have a good idea of your own. And remember, wedding presents can be given for up to a year following the wedding date, so take your time and think carefully about what the new couple would love to have.

◆ TIP ◆

For Ned and Nancy Newstart, the basics are always welcome. Couples with history or with previous marriages usually already have the basics, so something unusual or unexpected might be a good choice.

WEDDING PRESENTS

Leather overnight bag

Luggage, such as a wheelie with several zippered compartments

Leather photo album—have it engraved

Full-size vacuum cleaner

Portable handheld vacuum cleaner

Steam-or-dry iron

WEDDING PRESENTS

Handheld steamer (for removing creases)

Microwave oven

Toaster oven

Toaster

Percolator or countertop drip coffee pot (with filters)

Espresso or cappuccino maker, with small cups for espresso and large cups for cappuccino

Complete tea set: teapot, creamer, sugar bowl, honey pot, cups and saucers, small plates

WEDDING PRESENTS

"Smart" pot (Crock-Pot or slow-cooker)

Juicer

Set of vintage kitchen canisters

Three-tiered pedestal cake stand

Footed cake platter and dessert plates

Set of towels, bath mat, and matching
bathroom rug

Digital scale

Shower radio and CD player

Satin sheets—for the right couple

WEDDING PRESENTS

Set of sheets and pillowcases—the possibilities are many, from pure cotton to flannel or jersey, not to mention colors and patterns and pretty trimmings. Find out what the happy couple prefers.

Down pillows

Featherbed

Patchwork quilt

Cashmere throw

Angora blanket

Electric blanket

WEDDING PRESENTS

Tablecloth and napkins—these can be formal or informal: fine linen or damask in white, ivory, or a pastel; textured linen; cotton or cotton blend with a pattern or stripe, in bright, pastel, or deep colors.

Chrome (or other) pepper mill and salt shaker

Soup tureen and ladle

Country-look earthenware with painted, spatter, or sponge finish

Flatware or silverware in the couple's chosen pattern

Silver serving utensils

Serving bowl in china, glass, wood, chrome, copper

WEDDING PRESENTS

Stemware—wineglasses in several sizes, champagne flutes, brandy snifters

Glass pitcher and matching tumblers

Martini shaker and glasses

Ice bucket, with scoop or tongs

Wine rack

Case of good wine—either an assortment or a dozen bottles of one kind

Candlesticks in pewter, silver, gold, glass, etc.

Lead crystal—tumblers, bath accessories, bowl, etc.

Catalog Shopping

Catalog shopping has become a part of our lives, and a good thing, too. On-line or off, it's convenient, generally reliable, timesaving, and fun. The shipping costs sometimes make us think twice, but for gift giving, traveling the catalog route can be a smart way to go. You find the gift, order it, pay for it, have it gift wrapped, and send it, all in a matter of minutes.

It may surprise you to know that there's a catalog source for almost everything you could possibly think of. Go on-line, log on to your search engine, type in your keywords—*nostalgia candy* or *vintage cars* or *silk flowers* or *baseball bats* or whatever—and hit GO. Catalogs, stores, and all sorts of information will pop up for you to explore. Some sites will offer hard-copy catalogs, which you can order and browse through at home at your leisure; others are strictly on-line, and you can page through their goods screen by screen. And you can do all this in your spare moments between diaper changes, between meetings, between dinner and bedtime, or any other time.

◆ TIP ◆

No matter how obscure or oddball the gift you're looking for, chances are you'll find it on the Internet if you just keep searching. If you can't find what you want on a store or catalog site, try looking for it on one of the auction sites.

Anniversary Gifts

An anniversary gift can be anything you want it to be, but the tradition of tying each particular anniversary to a particular gift category is great fun and gives focus to the occasion. If you want to go along with tradition, here are plenty of ideas for each major anniversary—loosely interpreted so you'll have a little scope. There are also a handful of gift ideas applicable to any anniversary. Some gifts are for him to give *her*, some are for her to give *him*, and some are for anyone to give *them*.

Album of personal photos—this is a great one for kids to present to parents. Collect photos from as many years of the marriage as you can, put them into the album, and label with captions that tell where, when, who, and what was happening. Don't forget pix of relatives, parties, trips, outings, birthdays, and so on.

Family genealogy—have it done for the happy couple.

Dream-Come-True Gift—find out what his, her, or their dream is, and make it come true. Maybe it's a week in Paris, a ski trip, a poodle puppy, a strapless evening gown, Italian lessons, a backyard pool, or courtside seats at Wimbledon. Whatever it is, make it happen.

Surprise party

Weekend getaway—take him or her (or send *them*) off to a romantic weekend at an inn, hotel, or B-and-B. If there are kids involved, be sure they're in good hands for the entire weekend so the parents can relax and enjoy themselves.

First Anniversary: Paper

Collage of photos of the (relatively) new couple

Beautiful letterhead stationery with her name printed on it

Poster or fine-art print for the wall

Check or plenty of crisp green bills for spending any way at all

Tickets to a show, opera, classical concert, dance performance

Tickets to a sports event

Tickets to a pop concert

Plane tickets

Journal or diary

Love letters—as sweet, sentimental, and alluring as you can make them

Letter describing what you love and appreciate about your mate

Jar full of folded paper messages—promises, expressions of love, sexy invitations, etc.

Gift certificate to his, her, or their favorite store

Gift certificate for dinner at a fabulous restaurant

Special book: rare book, erotic book, novel by a favorite author (signed, if possible), first edition, etc.

New printer for the home office and lots of paper to go with it

Second Anniversary: Cotton

Supersoft sheets in a new and wonderful color

Flannel sheets

Hand-hooked or braided rug

Crocheted bedspread

Folk-art coverlet

ANNIVERSARY GIFTS

Pajamas, nightgown, nightshirt, robe

His-and-hers T-shirts with special messages printed on the front

Underwear printed with hearts or other romantic symbols

Huge towels for the beach

Place mats and matching napkins

Third Anniversary: Leather

Leather or suede jacket, vest, skirt, or pants

Leather-upholstered couch or lounge chair

ANNIVERSARY GIFTS

Briefcase or portfolio

Three pairs of suede gloves in three different colors

Cowboy boots

The shoes of her dreams

Fine leather handbag or tote

Baseball mitt

Leather-bound book, perhaps Shakespeare's sonnets or some other classic

Fourth Anniversary: Fruit or Flowers

Fruit- or flower-of-the-month club for a year

Lilac or hydrangea bush (or other flowering shrub)

Cherry or apple tree (or other fruit tree)

Collection of floral-scented soaps, lotion, bath oil, powder, cologne, candles, etc.

Wreath trimmed with dried flowers

Big bouquet of silk flowers

Cut-glass fruit bowl and set of fruit knives

Folk art depicting fruit and flowers—tole tray painted with flowers, still life painting done in naive style, carved wooden fruit, papier-mâché fruit, flower-painted furniture, flower-pattern or pineapple quilt

Trip to the country in wildflower season

Window box filled with geraniums or petunias

Glacé apricots, peaches, pears; white- and dark chocolate–dipped strawberries

Fifth Anniversary: Wood

Tree planted in their honor

Camping trip in the woods

Nested maple bowls

Set of Shaker chairs

Cedar chest

Handmade wooden Noah's ark or other folk art

Armoire or sideboard in a suitable style

Built-in wood cabinets for bedroom, den, or home office

Carved wood picture frame, and a piece of art or a photograph to go in it

Baseball bat—the best you can afford

ANNIVERSARY GIFTS

Tenth Anniversary: Tin or Aluminum

Punched-tin lanterns

Tins of caviar

Ten tins full of goodies: homemade cookies, candy, nuts, pretzels, and more

French aluminum cookware

Set of tin soldiers

Aluminum canoe

Fifteenth Anniversary: Crystal

Cut crystal punch bowl and cups

Decanter and brandy snifters

ANNIVERSARY GIFTS

Decorative ornaments such as animals, figures, small sculptures, etc.

Wristwatch, pocket watch, or pendant watch—the cover over the watch face is called a crystal!

Handsome piece of quartz crystal to use as a paperweight

Austrian crystal jewelry—earrings, bracelet, necklace

Crystal chandelier

Crystal ball for predicting the future

Evening dress or formal shirt with crystal pleating

Twentieth Anniversary: China

New pieces (bowls, serving platter, tureen, etc.) in their china pattern

Complete set of china in a fun new pattern

Turkey platter

Porcelain dessert plates and matching napkins

Porcelain soup bowls with saucers

Chinoiserie area rug

China cabinet

Trip to China

Dinner at a great Chinese restaurant

Course in Chinese cooking

Wok filled with Chinese cooking ingredients, plus a Chinese cookbook. Ingredients might include: soy sauce, hoisin sauce, Chinese mustard, five-spice powder, Chinese dried mushrooms, rice vinegar, sesame oil, dried noodles, fresh ginger, tea, bean sauce, Szechuan peppercorns, black beans, dried red chilies, star anise.

Twenty-fifth Anniversary: Silver

Jewelry for him or her—cuff links, watch, bracelet, necklace, earrings

Cocktail shaker, plus martini glasses

ANNIVERSARY GIFTS

Ice bucket and tongs

Etched silver tray

Bud vase

Monogrammed napkin rings

Basket of silver-colored fun things:
ribbon, wrapping paper, origami paper,
chocolate kisses, measuring spoons,
cookie cutters, small toy, silver pen, paper
clips, scissors, silver glitter, inexpensive
jewelry (hoop earrings, chains, bangles),
Christmas ornament, tinsel, candles,
party hats, paper plates, streamers,
and so on.

Silver mirror with silver frame

ANNIVERSARY GIFTS

Salt and pepper shakers

Carving set

Silver-backed hairbrush

Compact

His-and-hers engraved ID bracelets

Thirtieth Anniversary: Pearl

Classic pearl necklace or earrings

Black pearl necklace or earrings

Cuff links set with pearls

Compact, treasure box, or other small container inlaid with mother-of-pearl

Mother-of-pearl frame

Pearl-handled fruit or steak knives

Fortieth Anniversary: Rubies

Ruby glassware—tumblers, wine goblets, etc.

Ring or necklace set with a ruby

Ruby velvet throw pillows

Deep red rose bush

Japanese maple tree with deep red leaves

Case of Burgundy or Cabernet Sauvignon

Bottle of fine port—and some Stilton cheese to go with it

Big jar of candied cranberries

Crate of ruby-red grapefruits

Garden plants and feeders to attract ruby-throated hummingbirds

Fiftieth Anniversary: Gold

New gold wedding bands

Gold jewelry—cuff links, bracelet, earrings, necklace, pin

Gold watch

CD collection of golden oldies

ANNIVERSARY GIFTS

Anniversary cake with gold-leaf decorations

Beautiful piece of antique furniture with gold leaf finish

Trip to the Olympics to watch the athletes go for the gold

Gold-plated serving dishes, utensils, tray, etc.

Fifty gold-colored ornaments for the Christmas tree

Aquarium full of goldfish, plus all the accessories

Presents for Babies and New Moms and Dads

Babies—brand-new to the world of gifts—usually need everything. Even little Tiffany Thirdchild will still require plenty of worldly goods, which means you can't go too far wrong in whatever you choose. New moms and dads need things, too, so don't forget them in your enthusiasm for the adorable infant you can't wait to cuddle. They'll love you for it.

New Moms and Dads

Book on babies and child care

Memory book

Photo album

Picture frame for baby's photo

Baby carrier, front or back style

PRESENTS FOR BABIES AND NEW MOMS AND DADS

Jogging stroller

Diaper bag—tote style or backpack

Soft shawl or cozy robe, for night
feedings

Handprint or footprint kit for making
a keepsake

Babies

Stroller or carriage

Warm blanket for stroller or carriage—
homemade (knitted or crocheted) or
store-bought

Moses basket

Crib

Crib accessories: sheets, pillowcases, bumper, mobile (for hanging over the crib), soft mirror, bed skirt, quilt or comforter

Receiving blanket

Basic supplies—buy a nicely prepackaged selection or assemble a collection of your own, which might include cotton swabs, diapers, diaper pins, disposable diapers, thermometer, shampoo, baby soap, etc. Ask for advice at the baby store.

Basic layette—buy this as a complete package from a store or put it together on your own. It might include sleepers, body suits, T-shirts, gowns, and bibs.

Gift set—baby stores sell ready-to-go collections of baby items, often packaged in attractive baskets, totes, or diaper bags. The sets vary greatly, from simple to elaborate. And there's nothing to stop you from putting together a gift set of your own, working from this list:

- Feeding bottles and nipples
- Diapers
- Baby-care products, such as lotion, shampoo, massage oil, etc.
- Pacifier
- Baby T-shirts
- Hooded cover-up for after bath
- Soft towels and washcloths
- Bath toy
- Soft toy or stuffed animal
- Soft hand puppet

PRESENTS FOR BABIES AND NEW MOMS AND DADS

- ◆ Rattle or other sound-making toy
- ◆ CD of special music for baby

One-piece bunting, with or without hood

Cotton robe

Creeper

Playsuit or overalls

Sweater, with or without matching cap

Shirt and pants set

T-shirt and leggings set

Baby outfit, such as a fancy top and bloomers

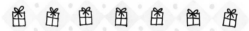

Little hangers for baby's outfits

Cap or hat in cotton, corduroy, soft wool, polyester, shearling. For a more substantial gift, add matching booties. If you knit or crochet, make a cap and booties yourself.

Socks and booties

Bibs—give several

PRESENTS FOR BABIES AND NEW MOMS AND DADS

Soft toy—blocks, doll, stuffed animal

Music box

Storybook—your old favorite or a more recent children's book

Early-development toys—there are dozens of possibilities here, so ask for a recommendation at the baby store. You might give a pull toy, blocks, music maker, stacking toy, play gym, balls, activity toy, books, walker, etc.

Indoor playhouse

Beach toys—pail, shovel, rake

PRESENTS FOR BABIES AND NEW MOMS AND DADS

Album with the baby's name embossed
on the cover

Silver cup or spoon—engraved, if you like

Brush and comb

Personalized dish and drinking cup

Get Help!

*S*o your heart is in the right place, you love giving gifts, yet somehow you're having trouble getting your feet to the store to pick out a cashmere sweater for Cousin Judy Faraway for Christmas. If that's the situation, *get help!* No, not therapy, just a great catalog on- or off-line so you can let your fingers do the walking. Don't you think Judy will love that pink cashmere sweater sent from a great catalog just as much as she'd love it if you went out, bought it yourself, wrapped it, and took the package to the post office? She'll probably love it more, because if you order from a catalog, chances are the sweater will get to Judy somewhere in the vicinity of Christmas—but if you do it yourself, good luck to

Judy. She'll probably be wearing cashmere and long sleeves in August.

There's no shame in getting help of any kind at all. Take advantage of catalog shopping (see page 130, too), franchised mailing services, gift wrapping and mailing at department stores, even personal shoppers, and get the job done.

Gifts for Young Kids

Kids vary widely in what they like and what they like to play with. Listen to what they tell you or ask their parents about it. And remember: What may be a simple toy for one kid may be a stretch for another, so choose carefully for the particular child.

◆ TIP ◆

The newest toy, the latest fad,
will make a kid happy—no matter how
silly the darned thing may seem to you.

Scooter

Wagon, such as the classic red wagon
or a wooden one

Tricycle or small two-wheeler

Kid-size car, motorcycle, or truck

Rocking horse

Toy vehicles—backhoe, dump truck, car, airplane, fire truck, ship

Electric train

Miniature toy cars

Robot or other action figure

Stuffed animal, large or small

Hand puppets or marionettes

Puppet stage or theater

Costume, such as ballerina, firefighter, cartoon or pop character, cowboy, police officer

GIFTS FOR YOUNG KIDS

Dress-up clothes—a box or trunk full of shoes, jewelry, hats, gloves, veil, scarves, skirts, etc., makes for hours and hours of imaginative fun for children. And none of the items need be brand-new or in perfect condition.

Dolls of all kinds, from soft stuffed ones to fancy costumed ones

Barbie and Barbie-type dolls and their outfits

Baby doll, baby crib, stroller, and other "baby" accessories

Doll clothes

Dollhouse and furniture

Doll's tea set

Wooden beads for stringing

Play-Doh, clay, or other similar sculpting material

Art supplies—in addition to the many ready-to-go sets of art supplies available, you can put together a set of supplies of your own choosing:

- ◆ Standing or tabletop easel, smock, tempera paints, brushes, paper
- ◆ Chalkboard, colored chalk, eraser
- ◆ Crayons and coloring book
- ◆ Colored pencils and sketchbook
- ◆ Markers and construction paper

Rubber stamps, plus inkpads in several colors

Stickers—the more variety, the better

Toy printing press

Child-size workbench and play tools—hammer, wrench, pliers, etc.

Play kitchen things—child-size appliances, fake food, pots and pans, apron and pot holders, chef's hat, dishes, etc.

Doctor or nurse gear

Basic chemistry set

Kid-size musical instrument, such as keyboard, xylophone, tambourine, drums

GIFTS FOR YOUNG KIDS

Wooden blocks

Construction toy with wood or metal pieces, joints, hinges, beams, rods, pulleys, motors

Simple jigsaw puzzle

Board game, such as Lotto or Candyland

Books—classics, best sellers, the newest picture books

Classic toy, such as Lego blocks or Lincoln Logs

Adventure-in-the-backyard set that includes kid-size binoculars, headlamps, flashlight, compass, canteen

Indoor or outdoor playhouse

Slumber bag—similar to a real sleeping bag and great for using on the bed or floor

Educational toys—to develop skills of all kinds, from building to reading

Walkie-talkie wristwatch

Piggy bank or other bank—and a handful of coins to put in it

Cash register

Funny mask

Toy chest—tuck a toy or two into it

Sheets and pillowcases printed with cartoon (or other) characters, or patterned in a sports theme, firefighter theme, etc.

Baseball cap with team logo

Firefighter-style waterproof raincoat, hat, and boots—bright yellow would be fun!

Child-size umbrella—in a pizzazzy color or pattern

Backpack—the coolest style you can find

Puppy, kitten, or other pet—only with parental permission, if you're not the parent!

Figuring Out
What to Give

Figuring out what gift to give an adult is actually quite easy in most cases. Take a look at his or her life—what do you see? For example, Roxie Cheerful's house is filled with plants; she adores bright colors; she wears oodles of different kinds of earrings; she loves contemporary fiction; she listens to jazz; she enjoys cooking and entertaining. Lots of gift-giving possibilities here: a flowering plant or other houseplant; a book on indoor gardening; a brightly colored scarf and matching hat; a brightly colored T-shirt or sweater; brightly colored dish towels, napkins, or placemats; sparkly earrings; antique earrings; the latest novel or short-story collection; a subscription to a literary magazine or book club; a variety of jazz CDs or a boxed set; half a dozen pillar candles in a bright color; a pretty serving platter; a new cookbook—and that's just the obvious stuff.

Let's try Jason Busyguy. He reads mysteries; he loves playing tennis; he roots for the Yankees; he's the cello in a chamber music group; he's crazy about Italian food; he travels for business. Quick—think of ten obvious gifts for Jason. See how easy that was?

Between your own observations and the lists in this book, you'll be able to come up with plenty of gift ideas for everyone in your life.

◆ TIP ◆

Another way to work this is to go the counterintuitive route. I have a woman friend whose dad always gives her "guy" stuff: jumper cables, a rechargeable lantern, tools. She loves it.

Gifts for Older Kids and Younger Teenagers

*I*n general, do *not* give clothes to older kids or younger teenagers—unless you want to reveal yourself to be as wrong-headed as Aunt Hortense Oldhat. *Things* are what this gang wants, and the cooler, the better.

◆ TIP ◆

Don't overlook tech stuff for this age group. See "Technogifts," page 273, for more ideas.

Motorized scooter

Battery-operated fold-up electric bike

Bicycle—be sure you get the right one

Sled—the fastest one you can find

Skateboard

Skates—for in-line skating, figure skating, or ice hockey

GIFTS FOR OLDER KIDS AND YOUNGER TEENAGERS

Stilts

Pogo stick

Trampoline—small for indoors, larger for outdoors

Sports equipment—see "Sports and Fitness Gifts," page 255, for lots of ideas.

Gift certificate for the latest sneakers or athletic shoes

Table-tennis set

Indoor bowling set

Kid-size pitching machine

GIFTS FOR OLDER KIDS AND YOUNGER TEENAGERS

Juggling balls

Magic set

Science kit for doing scientific experiments

Chemistry set

Microscope

Rocket-building kit

Pinhole photography kit

Magnet kit, with experiments

Dinosaur model kit or anything else on the subject of dinosaurs

Nature kit—this gift might relate to caterpillars, insects, ecology, geology, or frogs, for example, or it might be a kit for creating a terrarium or miniature indoor garden.

Anything connected to horses, for kids in love with horses—models, books, videos, etc.

Camping equipment—see "Outdoorsy Gifts," page 247, for lots of ideas.

Night-vision glasses or goggles

Headlamp, for camping, hiking, and general coolness

Backpack

GIFTS FOR OLDER KIDS AND YOUNGER TEENAGERS

Messenger bag

Computer and video games—the newest!

Favorite videos and DVDs

Table-style or pocket radio

Radio with headphones

Portable CD player

Gift certificate for CDs

Boom box

Headphones

Spy kit and spy equipment

GIFTS FOR OLDER KIDS AND YOUNGER TEENAGERS

Remote-controlled car, truck, robot, yacht, airplane, or helicopter

Kite—especially a really jazzy one

Clothing-design kit, including dolls, outfits, and decorations for the outfits

Scary mask

Challenging jigsaw puzzle

Board game

Labyrinth game—the classic wooden box with sliding steel balls

Chinese checkers

Musical instrument, such as guitar, recorder, electronic keyboard, drums, etc.

Karaoke machine

Craft set for making jewelry, doing enameling, trying glass painting, etc.

Stickers

Collage kit—if you want to put this together yourself in a cardboard or plastic box, consider including craft sticks, straws, pom-poms, chenille sticks, glitter, glitter pens, beads, doilies, feathers, yarn, buttons, sequins, spangles, stickers, etc. Add a pad of heavyweight bristol board or a few sheets of white poster board.

Art supplies—this gift might include paints (watercolor, acrylic, oil), brushes, pastels, colored pencils, markers, oil crayons, clay, watercolor paper, canvas board, sketchbook, etc.

Sheets and pillowcases in bright colors or patterns

School supplies: notebooks, pens, markers, etc.

Big poster of a favorite star, singer, or band

More Is Better

$\mathcal{I}$ went to sleepover camp for the first time when I was nine and, oh, it was so hard to be away from home! My father wrote letters, my aunt sent installments of *101 Dalmatians* clipped from a magazine, but my mother mailed shoe boxes wrapped in brown paper. Those boxes were life preservers—full of candy dots, Sugar Daddies, Chuckles, malt balls, red licorice strings, and little toys, too: jacks, colored chalk, a painted china dog, a tiny Kewpie doll.

Throughout this book you'll find suggestions for "more is better" gifts—gifts that include several (or more) items to

- eat—food samplers, gift baskets, candy assortments
- use—kitchen gadgets, craft supplies, desk accessories
- provide help—baby layette, organizers, travel essentials
- turn a house into a home—bed linens, table linens, stemware
- wear—hair ornaments, stack of T-shirts, slew of socks
- pamper—spa treats, skin care products, fragrance collections
- play with—puzzles, pets' toys, beach toys
- entertain—books, games, videos

These are just a few examples; there are lots more to choose from when less *isn't* more and more *is* better.

Gifts for Older Teens

Older teens, just a jot away from adulthood, love to get tech stuff, sports and fitness equipment, outdoor gear, cool clothes, and hot accessories, so be sure to check those categories (among others) for even more ideas than you'll find here.

◆ TIP ◆

Ask, ask, ask. Ask what she wants, ask what he longs for. These near-grown-ups usually know their own minds and will love you for probing them.

Gift certificate, off-line or on-line—it can be tricky to pick out a perfect gift for an older teen, so feel free to present him or her with a gift certificate or an e-gift certificate to a favorite store. Contrary to popular wisdom, *everyone* loves the luxury of choosing exactly what he or she wants! Off- or on-line stores to consider: clothing, accessories, makeup, book, tech, CD, video, sports equipment.

Cool clothes—the latest jeans, sweater, top, jacket, etc.

Cool shoes—the latest sneakers, running shoes, boots, etc.

T-shirts

Team gear—T-shirt, jacket, jersey, cap, etc.

School jacket

Class ring

Hot jewelry—the latest bracelet, earrings, necklace, watch, etc.

Sunglasses

Beach stuff: straw tote, beach towel, cover-up, flip-flops, bikini or other swimsuit

Scuba lessons

Disposable underwater camera

Racing bike

Scooter

Bike helmet

Bike chain and lock

Bike messenger bag

Backpack

Bookpack with lots of pockets and storage

Tabletop pool table and accessories

GIFTS FOR OLDER TEENS

Board game

Dartboard and darts

Skateboard

Snowboard

Ski stuff: skis, poles, boots, goggles, outerwear

Free weights

Exercise video or DVD

Favorite movie on video or DVD

TV for bedroom

Digital camera

GIFTS FOR OLDER TEENS

35mm single-lens-reflex camera, plus film

Disposable camera

Stereo speakers

Portable CD player

CDs—singles or a boxed set

Table-style or pocket radio

Notebook (or laptop) or desktop computer

Printer

Cell phone

GIFTS FOR OLDER TEENS

Beeper

Case for cell phone, beeper, etc.

Phone card

Prepaid wireless phone

Hands-free phone headset for driving

Six months' use of gasoline credit card

Concert tickets

Tickets to sports event

Gift certificate for movies

Subscription to a favorite magazine

Anything that relates to a special interest or hobby—this gift might be paints and brushes for an artist; a new guitar for a musician; software, storage, or scanner for a computer freak; chess set for a chess fan; tennis racket for an avid player; gym membership for a bodybuilder; new or classic novels for a budding writer.

Bedroom redecoration—redecorating can mean anything from a complete makeover to a simple change of bedspread or comforter with matching pillow shams or decorative pillows.

Desk and desk lamp

Grooming stuff: electric shaver, hair dryer or hot rollers, manicure products, etc.

Pampering stuff: bath salts, bath oil, bubble bath, body lotion, soap, facial mask, etc. (and see "Pampering Gifts," page 57, for more ideas)

Trendy cosmetics—see "Gifts for Looking and Feeling Attractive," page 33, for ideas.

Fragrance—cologne, purse spray, body lotion

Showing Appreciation

We live a *social* life, bumping up against one another constantly, muddling through with a little help from our friends—as well as our families, our neighbors, and a couple of dozen professionals at any given time. Which means there will be plenty of occasions when you'll want to acknowledge a kindness, a job well done, or a courtesy extended. Sometimes a simple (or lengthy!) spoken thank-you is sufficient. Sometimes it's not. Give a modest gift or remembrance to show your appreciation for:

- ◆ your child's teacher at the end of the year

- a business colleague who did you a small but meaningful favor
- the trainer at the gym, who's been so patient with you
- the friend who drove you home from bowling every week
- the neighbor who watched your house when you went away for a weekend
- the other neighbor who picked up your mail when you were out of town on business
- your best friend, after she spent two whole days helping you shop for that special dress
- your mother-in-law, for watching the kids four Saturdays in a row
- your father-in-law, for repairing the leak in the roof
- your sister, for being supportive just when you needed her most

Housewarming Presents

Every new move—to apartment, town house, fixer-upper, farm, or mansion—deserves to be celebrated with a gift when you visit for the first time. A small gift is completely appropriate; you need not go overboard. It really is the thought that counts.

HOUSEWARMING PRESENTS

Bread and salt—a traditional house-warming gift, which can be interpreted in many ways—perhaps with a crusty round loaf ribbon-tied to a breadboard, accompanied by a salt mill and a box of sea salt.

Photo album and disposable camera—take some pictures of the day you visit.

Guest book

Linen guest towels—monogrammed, if you like

Welcome mat—choose one printed with the word *welcome*.

HOUSEWARMING PRESENTS

Wreath for the front door, trimmed with natural materials, dried flowers, berries, etc.

Beautiful basket or two

Arrangement of silk or dried flowers

Vase or bud vase

Decorative pillow—choose silk, velvet, brocade, corduroy, cotton print or stripe, or embroidered fabric. It's fun to give a stack of three pillows, tied together with ribbon.

Bag of fresh coffee beans or ground coffee

Jam sampler (three different kinds), plus a glass or china jam jar

HOUSEWARMING PRESENTS

Honey jar, wooden honey server, and honey

Fancy teabags

Teapot

Teakettle

Set of mugs

Set of kitchen canisters, to match kitchen decor or color

HOUSEWARMING PRESENTS

Dish towels and pot holders

Pair of oven mitts

Pair of trivets

Kitchen clock

Kitchen gadgets—see "Gifts for the Cook," page 217.

Salad bowl and servers

Steak knives

Serving tray, perhaps tole, wood, or rattan

Tablecloth

Place mats

HOUSEWARMING PRESENTS

Cloth napkins and pretty napkin rings

Corkscrew—and a bottle of wine, if you like

A dozen (or more) tall tapered candles in bright or pastel colors

Several pillar candles, scented or not

Paper lanterns for stringing across a patio or yard

One or two hurricane lamps, with appropriate candles

Feather duster, with real feathers

Bedside clock

HOUSEWARMING PRESENTS

Cedar hang-ups or disks

Shower radio

Over-the-tub bath caddy

Birdhouse or bird feeder

Wind chimes

Hanging planter, with or without a plant

Intangible Gifts

$\mathcal{D}$oing a good deed or a favor for someone is another way of giving a gift—an intangible one, to be sure, but a gift nonetheless. And often your intangible gift will have a more lasting effect than any tangible one could.

- ◆ Make a connection for a colleague, to a businessperson or someone else in a position to give advice or assistance.

- ◆ Help a friend clean up and organize her garage, attic, closet, kitchen, or desk.

- ◆ Do a chore (or two chores) for someone who's coping with a family problem—shop for groceries, pick up the kids at school, make phone calls, prepare a meal.

- Teach your mother, aunt, or grandmother to use her new computer.

- Introduce a child to a famous or accomplished person you happen to know—a sports figure, writer, actor, scientist, inventor.

- Volunteer to do something useful—deliver meals to homebound folks, serve food at a soup kitchen, work at a charity thrift shop, read to a blind person, visit the elderly or sick.

- Take a child to a museum, aquarium, planetarium, art gallery, or library.

- Share your special skill with a friend—teach her to knit or crochet, bake a cake, plant a garden, mend a sock, fix a faucet, drive a car.

Host and Hostess Gifts

Whether you're spending an evening, a weekend, or a week, a gift to your host and hostess is a way of showing your appreciation for the time and effort they've taken to make you welcome on the occasion of your visit. The length of your stay at their home generally dictates the size of the gift, and you may bring it with you or send it later (as you would a thank-you note).

HOST AND HOSTESS GIFTS

Flowers—bouquet of something special, such as roses, freesias, lilies, or gladioli (if you're bringing it with you), or a seasonal or mixed bouquet (when sending it later from a florist)

Large vase or several bud vases

Houseplant—a flowering plant or something lush and green

Pot of paperwhites, other narcissi, amaryllis, or tulips

Bottle of wine, champagne, or liqueur

Martini, margarita, or liqueur glasses, or other fun stemware

HOST AND HOSTESS GIFTS

Wine carafe

Place mats and matching napkins

Large or small gift basket: cheese and
biscuits, coffee and tea, nuts and snacks,
candies, condiments (mustard, hot
sauce, chutney, etc.), jams and jellies

Basket of tropical or exotic fruit,
such as pineapple, mangos, papayas,
kumquats, etc.

Basket of apples, pears, and figs, with
an appropriate cheese or two

Cheese, cheese board, cheese knife

Bakery goodies—such as cookies, fruit
tarts, éclairs, pound cake, layer cake, etc.

HOST AND HOSTESS GIFTS

Fresh coffee beans or ground coffee
(if you know what kind of coffeemaker
they use)

Special food treat, such as caviar, pâté,
English toffee, chocolate coffee beans,
chocolate truffles, gourmet cocoa,
cheese straws, a regional specialty,
your own homemade specialty (cookies,
jam, chutney, salsa, pesto, and so on)

Assortment of spices, herbs, herb blends

Pepper grinder and peppercorns

Pizza stone and pizza cookbook

Wok, wok accessories, and a book about
Chinese cooking

HOST AND HOSTESS GIFTS

Demitasse set

Personalized mugs

Interesting serving piece, perhaps a sectioned relish dish, bowl, large platter, handsome painted tray, etc.

Fancy soaps

Set of pretty fingertip (guest) towels

Votive candleholders and candles

Large or small hurricane lamps with candles to fit inside

Several pillar candles in bright colors

Latest novel or short-story collection

HOST AND HOSTESS GIFTS

Coffee-table book—choose a book about a subject that interests your host and hostess—their state or city, a place they love (or would love) to visit, the work of an artist they admire, American or Civil War history, English gardens, an architectural style, antiques, rock and roll, Hollywood stars, etc.

Board game, dominoes, blackjack or poker set

Something seasonal—see "Seasonal Gifts," page 99.

Photo album

Favorite movie (or two) on video or DVD

Gifts for the Cook

Novice or veteran, anyone who voluntarily spends time in the kitchen loves the gear and special ingredients that go with cooking. Match the gift to the level of experience (or aspiration), the space available for storing new equipment, and the particular culinary interests of the cook in question.

GIFTS FOR THE COOK

Cooking lessons—pay for your favorite cook to take a series of cooking classes, a one-day workshop, or even private lessons. He or she might learn a favorite cuisine (Italian, Thai, Indian, etc.), a special skill (cake or bread baking, pasta making, etc.), or how to prepare a specific menu.

Wine-appreciation course

Full-size or mini food processor

Convection oven

Electric warming tray

Outdoor grill

Hibachi

GIFTS FOR THE COOK

Grilling tools—brush, tongs, spatula, fork, skewers

Espresso or cappuccino maker

Pasta machine

Bread machine

Waffle iron

Deep fryer

Pressure cooker

Countertop or handheld electric mixer

Blender

Electric food grinder

A Gift You Can't Gift Wrap

This sort of gift isn't a *thing,* it's an *occasion* or *experience.* It might be as simple as a picnic in the country or as jazzy as a whitewater-rafting expedition. You might, for example, know that Mike Wishful has always wanted to soar over the fields in a hot-air balloon. Arrange for him to do it, then present him with a helium-filled balloon tied with ribbon, and a handwritten card that explains what the gift is, when it can be claimed, and where to claim it.

◆ TIP ◆

Bungee-jumping, waterskiing, tickets for the Westminster dog show, a trip to a fashion show, a day at the races, a night on the town, a surprise party—whatever your gift comprises, it should always be an experience you're sure the recipient *wants,* rather than an experience you think the recipient *should have.*

Rice cooker

Food dehydrator

Smoker

Ice cream maker

Juicer

Complete set of knives, including paring, boning, and chef's knives, serrated slicer, plus a sword-style sharpener

GIFTS FOR THE COOK

Carving set

Collection of kitchen gadgets—this gift might include several of the following: peeler, handheld grater, egg slicer, measuring spoons and cups, small and large spatula, wooden spoons, corkscrew, garlic press, wire whisk, oven thermometer, kitchen scissors, lemon squeezer, basting brush.

Kitchen scale

Three-channel timer

Pot holders and dish towels

Enameled cast-iron cookware

Roasting pan and rack

High-quality sauté pan, saucepan and lid, stockpot, fry pan

Nonstick frying pan plus nonscratching utensils (spatula, spoons, etc.)

Wok and wok utensils

General bakeware, for novice or aspiring bakers: cookie sheets, cookie press, cookie cutters, cake pans, loaf pans, pie pans, muffin tins, simple Bundt pan, popover pan

Special bakeware, for experienced or ambitious bakers: fancy ring mold or Bundt pan; special baking pans for buns, madeleines, baguettes, scones, mini-cakes, etc.

GIFTS FOR THE COOK

Pie baker's gear—put together this collection for someone who's learning (or wants to learn) to bake pies: two metal or glass pie pans, rolling pin, pastry cloth, pie cutter, pastry blender, brush, and your own favorite pie recipes or pie cookbook.

Cake or cookie decorating set

Two cookie jars—one for soft cookies, one for crisp cookies

High-quality pepper mill and peppercorns

Salt mill and package of coarse sea salt

Food mill

Nested stainless steel or glass bowls

GIFTS FOR THE COOK

Classic bean pot

Classic onion-soup bowls with lids

Mortar and pestle

Garlic roaster

Fine olive oil

Selection of vinegars, such as balsamic, sherry, rice wine, etc.

Selection of spices and herbs

Bottles of pure extracts—vanilla, lemon, orange, almond, peppermint

High-quality chocolate or cocoa for baking

Heavy canvas tote for marketing

GIFTS FOR THE COOK

Apron—the classic chef style in white, blue denim, or a pretty color

Blank recipe book, with a few of your favorite recipes written into it to get the book started

Cookbook stand, for keeping any cookbook open to the recipe in use

Gifts of Time, Relief, and Respite

Gifts aren't always things you can literally put your fingers on. Sometimes they're about providing comfort, care, relief, or respite—providing something the recipient can't or won't give herself, something that would simply make her feel better, or something that allows her much-needed time for herself. If you know someone who needs a helping hand, reach out and give her one of these:

◆ Handmade coupon redeemable for:

   ◆ a few hours of baby-sitting so she (or they) can have an afternoon or evening off

   ◆ an evening of reading aloud

- three mornings of ironing, food shopping, laundry, or any other chore
- a home-cooked meal every night for a week
- help with yard work
- help with paperwork
- Car service (you!) to visit family or a dear friend
- Professional massage
- Facial
- Manicure and/or pedicure
- Whole day at a spa
- Afternoon of clothes shopping
- Lunch—and a sympathetic ear
- Phone call to ask how she's doing and tell her you care

Craft and Hobby Gifts

Anyone with a passion for a craft or hobby is lucky, and so is the friend or relative who wants to give him or her a gift. Just take a moment to check up on what new supplies or tools are on the hobbyist's wish list—bingo, there's the right present.

◆ TIP ◆

Don't give a craft or hobby gift to Trixie Allthumbs or Max Verybusy. She or he will look at the gift with dismay, pretend to love it, and eventually donate it to the Salvation Army.

Ready-made kits—the kit possibilities are many: models (such as airplanes), papercraft, beading, needlepoint, crewel, cross-stitch, mosaic, ribboncraft, flower craft, candles, decoupage, dollhouse, doll, leather, origami, wood carving, batik, stained glass, soap making, enameling, jewelry, weaving, quilting, rug hooking, fabric painting, glass painting.

Homemade kits—put together a kit of your own by gathering the supplies needed for any of the crafts mentioned above; the salesperson at the art- or craft-supply store will help you find what you want. Package the items in a sturdy box or basket and wrap nicely.

Tools—choose high-quality or inexpensive tools—one, a few, or many—and consider giving a carrying case, too.

Multitool—this useful gadget is a sort of handle with many attached tools (screwdriver, pliers, wire cutter, scissors, etc.) that fold away. Great for car, apartment, or boat.

Electric drill, cordless or with cord

Circular saw

Glue gun and supply of glue inserts

Dremel kit with lots of bits and attachments

Albums for collections such as stamps, dried flowers, or stickers

Scrapbook and scrapbook supplies

Blank cards, plus glitter pens, markers, and stickers—for making greeting cards

Calligraphy pens, ink, and fine paper

Wine journal or record book

Chess set

CRAFT AND HOBBY GIFTS

Beer-making kit

Knitting and crocheting supplies: pattern book; special yarn; needles, hooks, and other tools; how-to book on fancy stitches, etc.

Sewing machine

Sewing scissors or pinking shears

Embroidery thread, canvas, needles

Needlepoint canvas (preprinted or not), plus yarn and needles

Clay and modeling tools—and a few classes in clay modeling, too

Paints, brushes, and other fine art accessories—if you're not familiar with these supplies, ask a salesperson to help you put your gift together. Choose supplies for oil or acrylic painting, watercolors, or gouache.

Easel—fancy or simple, indoor or outdoor

Stencils and stencil supplies

Glass paint, plus brushes and other accessories

Faux-finishing kit—there's a great variety of finishes to choose from: marbling, antiquing, crackling, etc.

Flower press

Musical Gifts

The sound of music is a joy to most folks and therefore has the makings of a perfect gift. If you're giving actual music—CDs, tapes, tickets to a concert—find out what the recipient really likes to listen to (Sylvia Symphony is *not* going to enjoy the same music that Ricky Hiphop or Willy Bluesman enjoys). And never give a set of drums to a child without getting the okay from his parents first.

MUSICAL GIFTS

Instrument—anything from an alpenhorn to a zither

Sheet music

Songbook

Vocal or orchestral score

Music stand

Metronome

CDs

Tapes

Vintage (vinyl) records

MUSICAL GIFTS

Complete recorded works of a favorite singer, songwriter, band, composer, lyricist, or musician

Tickets to a concert—classical, rock, chamber music, folk, world music, gospel, etc.

Subscription to concert series or opera season

Tickets to a Broadway or touring musical

Portable CD player

CD rack or other CD storage device for the home

CD storage case for the car

MUSICAL GIFTS

CD carrying case

Boom box

Full-size or portable stereo

Speakers

Headphones

Biography of a favorite composer or performer

Book on the history of jazz, rock, folk, or other musical style

Coffee-table book about Broadway or film musicals, rock stars, rock groups, the Beatles, etc., with lots of great photographs

Karaoke machine

Music box

A day at a recording studio, for making a disc of his or her own songs or any other music

A trip to Nashville

A trip to La Scala

Serenade—hire a trio to croon outside your true love's window, or have the roving mariachi band (or gypsy violinist) visit your table when you take her to that special restaurant.

Dinner at a restaurant that has a terrific pianist, or a night out at a piano bar

MUSICAL GIFTS

Dinner or drinks at a great jazz club or country-and-western hangout

Player piano and rolls

Electronic keyboard or digital drum pads

Fun-and-Games Gifts

These are presents that provide entertainment, amusement, laughs, diversion,
and a rollicking good time. Buy some for
yourself, too.

FUN-AND-GAMES GIFTS

Comedy videotape or DVD—look for a funny movie (old or new), performance by favorite comedian, collection of episodes of favorite TV program, TV comedy special (contemporary or vintage).

CDs of great dance music—get up and shake that thing!

Home movies converted to videotape

Gift certificate for a year's worth of movies at a local theater

Jigsaw puzzles—choose complicated puzzles that will challenge the whole family.

Board games—choose a classic such as Scrabble, Monopoly, chess, checkers, dominoes, Trivial Pursuit, Boggle, or backgammon, or choose the latest popular game. If you don't know what the newest games are, inquire at your local toy store or large bookstore.

Jigsaw puzzles—choose complicated puzzles that will challenge the whole family.

Book of card games—learn to play something new.

Book of solitaire games

Electronic game: solitaire, bridge, chess, crossword puzzles, etc.

FUN-AND-GAMES GIFTS

Trip to Las Vegas, Reno, Atlantic City, or any other casino empire

Pinball machine

Humor book by a funny writer, book on a funny topic, or a book of jokes or cartoons

Electronic book of jokes

Tickets to a Broadway comedy, or one off-Broadway, off-off Broadway, or at your regional theater

Tickets to see the performance of a favorite comedian

Night out at a comedy club

Outdoorsy Gifts

$\mathcal{P}$art of the fun of doing outdoor activities is being properly (and coolly) equipped. Give your favorite outdoorsperson something wonderful to enjoy on the mountain, the beach, the water, or the trail, or in the woods, fields, or jungles. Keep in mind that this list may not include what's needed for your giftee's outdoor sport of choice (scuba diving? triathlon?), so think creatively, using the list for inspiration.

OUTDOORSY GIFTS

Pocketknife with lots of gadgets

Pocket multitool, with scissors, screw-drivers, etc.

Binoculars

Tent

Hiking boots (or gift certificate for them)

Hiking poles

Sleeping bag

Sleeping pad (to go under the sleeping bag)

Soft-pack cooler, small or large

Camp lantern plus batteries

OUTDOORSY GIFTS

Daypack for short hikes or day trips, or for carrying sports gear

Backpack for long trips

Backpacking stove

Pack towels and biodegradable soap

Shortwave radio

Two-way radio

Global positioning system (GPS) unit

Expedition watch—with chronometer, alarm, timer, time zone trackers

Altimeter watch

OUTDOORSY GIFTS

Sunglasses that filter out 100 percent of UV and IF rays

Wide-mouth, one-liter water bottle

Foldable water carrier

First-aid kit

Survival kit

"Possible" kit—put this one together yourself, to cover your favorite out-doorsperson in a slew of "possible" situations: sunscreen, ibuprofen, police-style whistle on lanyard, compass, lighter, waterproof firestick, shrink-wrapped space blanket, iodine tablets for water purification, emergency food.

Outerwear—give something that serves for a variety of activities or something specifically suited to a particular climate, place, or activity: fleece vest; zippered canvas or nylon jacket; down jacket, coat, or parka; superwarm hat; high-tech waterproof mittens or gloves; broad-brimmed sun hat; jeans lined with cotton flannel or polyester fleece; special socks to wear with hiking boots, ski boots, or running shoes; traditional hunting jacket or field coat of cotton canvas trimmed with corduroy, with or without a lining.

Washable silk underwear—long-sleeve top, long bottoms, etc.

Driving gloves

Snowshoes and poles

OUTDOORSY GIFTS

Giant beach ball

Inflatable water toy

Swimming-pool game, such as volleyball

Croquet set

Boccie set

Horseshoe set

Fly rod and reel

Fly box, rod bag, reel case

OUTDOORSY GIFTS

Fishing vest

Waders

Canoe, collapsible or not

Kayak, collapsible or not

Boating-trip supplies—big sponge for bailing, dry bags in a few sizes, dry suit, etc.

Skis or gift certificate for skis—cross-country, Alpine touring, downhill

Water skis or gift certificate for water skis

Riding boots

Saddlebags

Snowboard

Ice skates—figure, speed, hockey, or all-purpose

In-line skates

Sports and Fitness Gifts

Happily, there are more sports and fitness activities than could possibly be covered here, so if there's something special and different your gift recipient loves to do, find out what she needs and give it to her.

◆ TIP ◆

Don't forget Mr. and Mrs. Loyalfan, who sit in the bleachers and cheer— they need presents, too.

Membership in a gym

One or more sessions with a private trainer

Membership in a weight-loss or other fitness program

Membership at a Y that has a pool, fitness classes, squash court, etc.

Fitness or exercise tape—choose anything from yoga, tai chi, or kickboxing to Pilates, dance aerobics, or step workouts.

Portable CD player or radio, with headphones

Home-gym equipment

SPORTS AND FITNESS GIFTS

Portable stepper machine

Stationary bicycle

Treadmill

Set of hand weights

Set of padded ankle weights

Step bench (for step aerobics)

Exercise tubing or bands

Exercise ball

Jump rope

Yoga mat

SPORTS AND FITNESS GIFTS

Yoga outfit—long or Capri pants, plus soft or clingy top; be sure what you buy is stretchy and comfortable

Pullover sweatshirt and sweatpants

Zippered sweatshirt, with or without hood

Warm-up knits

Spandex top and pants or shorts

Stylish workout clothes: tights, leotard, unitard, stretchy top, cover-up, etc.

Team jersey or jacket

Team T-shirt

Medium or small duffel for gym

SPORTS AND FITNESS GIFTS

Biking glasses

New bike seat—padded, high-tech, etc.

AM-FM bike radio that attaches to handlebars

Aluminum sports bottle, with or without a carrying sling

Helmet—for biking, skiing, snowboarding, etc.

Mask and snorkel set

Foot fins

Water-fitness (aqua aerobics) equipment—buoyancy belt, weights, or special shoes

Running watch

Pedometer

Pitching machine

Lacrosse stick

Basketball

Baseball or softball equipment, such as bat, ball, or mitt

Volleyball

Golf equipment—clubs, lightweight pull cart, golf bag, golf scope

Bowling ball

SPORTS AND FITNESS GIFTS

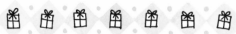

Bowling shoes

Boxing gloves

Indoor skates

Tennis racket and balls

Tennis outfit

Gift certificate for table time at a local pool hall

Padded stadium cushion

Waterproof stadium blanket

Thermos

The Token That Tells the Tale

When you're giving something that will actually take place at a future time (such as a subscription to the opera or a weekend at a country inn) or something that has yet to be delivered, picked up, or chosen (major appliance, furniture, puppy, winter coat), how will you convey the gift message to your loved one? Easy—by giving a token that tells (or hints at) what the gift is, along with a handwritten card that explains the details. Here are some suggestions for gifts and their possible tokens:

- Subscription to the opera: CD of one of the scheduled operas
- Tickets to the ballet: tiny ballerina made of china or glass
- Magazine subscription: rolled-up copy of the magazine, wrapped and tied with ribbon

- Weekend in the country: nosegay of wild-flowers; autumn leaves tied with ribbon; map with the route to the inn marked out and a big X at the inn's location; picture of the inn cut from its brochure and tucked into an inexpensive frame
- Dinner at a great restaurant: menu (or matchbook) from the chosen restaurant; a review of the restaurant, clipped from a newspaper or magazine and glued into a bright red folder
- Trip to Paris or anywhere else: miniature Eiffel Tower or other landmark evocative of the destination; piece of doll-size luggage with a tag naming the destination; toy airplane
- New car: model of the same car; model of a vintage car
- Appliance or furniture: dollhouse-size replica of whatever the gift is
- Puppy or kitten: stuffed animal; china or glass animal
- Winter coat or other clothing: doll-size coat, jacket, or whatever the gift is

Presents for Pets and Their Owners

Gifts for pets should be chosen with pet *and* owner in mind. Take into account the age, energy, and activities of the pet, as well as how recently the pet was acquired. A brand-new pet or owner, just like a brand-new baby or parent, might like to receive the basics rather than the extras.

Dog, cat, or other pet—needless to say, be careful with this one—be sure the animal is a welcome gift. Consider adopting a rescue animal, too.

Book on pet care

Book on a specific breed of animal

Book of photographs of pets or a specific kind of pet

Pet calendar

Pet grooming supplies, such as comb, nail clippers, brush, shampoo, etc.

PRESENTS FOR PETS AND THEIR OWNERS

Enamel or ceramic bowl for food and water

Leash or lead

Pet bed—choose a round, square, or pouch-style bed in plain denim, fleece, or any other sturdy fabric. Look for a removable cover with an odorproof cushion inside.

Heated pet bed

Pet first-aid kit

Collar or harness for dog or cat

ID tag for collar

Toy—what you pick depends on the pet, of course. Consider a soft, plush, or squeaky toy; ball, bone, or fetch toy; furry mouse or catnip toy; or other toy specific to the animal or breed.

Doggie panniers—a great gift if the dog goes on camping trips, so he can carry his own food

Foldable dog bowl, for trips and camping

Pet carrier or tote

Pet pouch—wearable (like a Snugli), for small- to medium-size dogs

Car seat

Heated pet blanket for car trips

PRESENTS FOR PETS AND THEIR OWNERS

Gourmet dog biscuits or other pet treats

Doggie coat

Anything with a dog or cat (or other animal) theme: needlepoint pillow, lamp, snow globe, jewelry, T-shirt, sweatshirt, eyeglass case, mug, stationery, etc.

Fish, fish tank, fish food, and other accessories

Decorative items for fish tank

Supply of pet food

Bird feeder and bird food

Birdcage

Bird treats

The Art of the Gift Certificate

Here comes a little test question. True or false: I really hated receiving that gift certificate from my favorite store.

No-brainer, right? Contrary to what *some* people say, gift certificates are neither impersonal nor unwelcome. Think what fun it is to find a twenty-dollar bill on the sidewalk, yours to spend—unexpectedly—in any way you like. That's the fun of receiving a gift certificate: You can choose whatever you like best. That's the joy of giving one, too: You allow your giftee to have the pleasure of getting *exactly* what he wants most.

Even when you give a gift certificate—an "unchosen" gift—you still have to choose the store or catalog (off- or on-line) from which it should come, so be savvy when you pick: Don't give Harry Stayat-home a gift certificate from a sporting-equipment store if he loves to sit by the fire and read. Don't give Jennifer Rough-houser a gift certificate from a fancy clothing shop if she lives in jeans and sweatshirts. Don't give Mr. and Mrs. Workovertime a gift certificate from a baby boutique if they're completely career-tracked. Use the same good judgment you'd use when picking any gift.

◆ TIP ◆

Consider giving a gift certificate for something that's not, in fact, a *thing*: spa services, massage, tickets to the movies, time at a sports facility, haircut or styling, makeup makeover, restaurant meal, language or cooking class, tennis lessons, tango lessons, driving lessons, even car washes.

Technogifts

Something for everyone here—even for the person who thinks she's a technophobe, not a technophile. You can be sure a new TV or cordless phone will delight even the most low-tech type, while the latest whiz-bang *digital* anything should make a high-tech fan jump for joy.

◆ TIP ◆

Loads of new items are coming out all the time. Check the stores and on- and off-line catalogs for the latest stuff for your favorite techie.

Disposable camera

Classic point-and-shoot camera and film

Digital camera

Binoculars

Digital camcorder or Palmcorder

Camcorder bag

Editing kit for camcorder

Tripod

Telescope

TECHNOGIFTS

Favorite movie, TV series, or documentary on videotape or DVD

Home-theater system

Pocket or portable radio featuring AM-FM, stereo, minidisc or cassette player, etc.

Microcassette recorder

Blank audiotapes or videotapes

Portable CD or DVD player

DVD or CD recorder

MP3 player

Hi-fi stereo VCR

Desktop audio system

TECHNOGIFTS

High-quality headphones, with or without cord

Clock radio—CD player combo

Notebook (or laptop) computer

Carrying case for notebook computer

Desktop computer

Flat-panel computer monitor

Zip drive or other computer data-storage system

Computer keyboard

Mini vacuum for computer

TECHNOGIFTS

Computer headset or earbud system

Ink-jet or laser printer, plus extra ink cartridges

Scanner

Handheld computer or pocket PC

Computer game and controller

Software—think creatively about subject matter here: accounting, languages, interactive educational, fantasy games, desktop publishing, screenwriting, graphics and drawing, hobbies, encyclopedia, and so on.

Calculator

TECHNOGIFTS

Cordless phone

Telephone headset

Fax machine

Combined phone and fax machine

Digital answering machine

Personal copier

Newest TV

Small TV for kitchen, office, etc.

Handheld TV

PDA (personal digital assistant)—the latest model, the one with the most features, or perhaps the one that's easiest to use

TECHNOGIFTS

Leather PDA holder

Handheld personal entertainment organizer

Handheld electronic game

Electronic reference units—language translator, dictionary, thesaurus, weather info, etc.

Global positioning system (GPS) unit

Shortwave radio

Two-way radio

The Gift of Tradition, History, and Memory

$\mathcal{S}$hiny new gifts are fun to get, of course, but there's something special, even thrilling, about receiving a gift that's infused with meaning because of its history or the memories it evokes. My own favorite was a single diamond, one of three removed from a ring of my grandmother's, which my mother had a jeweler set into a new ring especially for me. Instant history, instant memory of my Grandma Celia, every time I wear the ring.

A set of dishes or silverware, a wedding ring, a watch, a treasured piece of furniture, Aunt Nina's handwritten recipes in their original box—anything that reminds you of a loved one (living or not) or gathers you into the ongoing tradition of your family is an honor to own and care for. Keep it safe and pass it on.

Gifts to Please Anyone with an Office

We spend a lot of time in our offices (either at home or away from home) so anything that makes office life more pleasant or efficient will be a true gift. Here's where a slightly more extravagant present may be really appreciated, too—especially for a person who has recently set up a home office, gone into business for herself, or gotten a promotion and a new office to go with it. But your gift doesn't *have* to be large: A good supply of his favorite rollerball pens could be a welcome sight to Bobby Newjob.

Calendar for wall or desk

Business cards

Letterhead and matching envelopes

Personalized memo pads or notepads

Mini refrigerator

Microwave oven

Electric coffeemaker or teakettle

Portable fan for desktop

Clock radio–CD player combo

Cordless telephone

Phone with answering machine

Answering machine

Fax machine

Combined fax and phone machine

Desk accessories, such as desk pad, business-card holder, pen cup, "in" box, paper-clip holder, letter opener, memo-pad holder, etc.

Desk organizers, such as stacking paper trays, file storage boxes, boxes with compartments for pens and clips, drawer organizer, etc.

Office tools: stapler, scissors, ruler, paper punch, tape dispenser, etc.

Office supplies: pens, pencils, markers, index cards, tape, labels, memo pads, message pads, staples, printer paper, file folders, expanding envelopes, paper clips, pushpins, rubber bands, plain and manila envelopes, padded envelopes, stamps, stick-on notes, etc.

Electric or battery-powered pencil sharpener

Cassette recorder and cassettes

Rolodex (or similar) file

File cabinet

Comfortable desk chair

Desk lamp

GIFTS TO PLEASE ANYONE WITH AN OFFICE

Desktop computer

Notebook (or laptop) computer

Zip drive or other computer data-storage system

Business, graphics, or reference software

Mouse pad

Wrist rests

Printer

Scanner

Personal copier

Chalkboard and chalk

Gifts for Your Business or Professional Connections

These gifts can be a little tricky. You generally want to give something that's not too personal (since this is a business relationship) but still shows your appreciation for the recipient. And you have to consider the price—should you give a token gift or a substantial one? If your company has guidelines or a policy about gift giving, then you'll know how to handle this; if you're in doubt about what's appropriate to give to whom, ask for advice from others in your business or profession. The list that follows includes a wide variety of gifts, ranging from the inexpensive to the extravagant.

GIFTS FOR YOUR BUSINESS
OR PROFESSIONAL CONNECTIONS

Gift baskets, boxes, and tins—choose a basket that you're certain the recipient will enjoy (no wine for a nondrinker or smoked turkey for a vegetarian). And give a thought to style: An elegant box of very special chocolates may be right for Marla Sophisticate; a big basket of cheese, sausage, nuts, and hot sauce would be best for Harry Goodoldboy. Here are a few ideas:

- ◆ Wine and cheese
- ◆ Fresh fruit and candy
- ◆ Cakes, cookies, and other sweets
- ◆ Combination of foods, such as smoked meats, pâtés, cheeses, crackers, fruit, nuts, etc.
- ◆ Chocolates and other special candies
- ◆ Dried or glacé fruits, such as apricots, pineapple, pears, dates, etc.

GIFTS FOR YOUR BUSINESS
OR PROFESSIONAL CONNECTIONS

- ◆ Regional specialties
- ◆ Jams, jellies, and conserves

Wine duffel

Flowers or a special plant, such as an orchid or bonsai tree

Cashmere scarf

Cuff links

Watch

Small travel clock

World-time digital alarm clock

World-band radio

AM-FM pocket radio

Jogger's radio

Commuter's mug

Travel cart

Personalized luggage tags

Leather items—there are many to choose from: photo wallet, credit card case, business card holder, travel-document holder, zippered portfolio, pad holder, CD case, bound journal, ring binder, wallet, playing-card case, monogrammed key case, address book, etc.

Attaché case or briefcase

Computer case or bag

GIFTS FOR YOUR BUSINESS OR PROFESSIONAL CONNECTIONS

Desktop computer light that fastens to the top of a monitor

Magnifying glass

Paperweight—choose a special style, such as one made of Murano glass.

Fountain pen or other fine writing instrument

High-tech (but inexpensive) pen

Pen and pencil set

Fancy mouse pad

Personal desktop fan

Lap desk

Matching desk accessories, such as a desk pad, business-card holder, pen cup, "in" box, clock, paper-clip holder, letter opener, memo or notepad holder, etc.

Electronic dictionary or translator

Electronic organizer or PDA

Handheld (pocket) PC

Calculator

Mini tool kit

GIFTS FOR YOUR BUSINESS
OR PROFESSIONAL CONNECTIONS

Home and auto tool kit

Mini chess or checkers set

Handheld puzzles

Book about the city or region in which
the giftee lives

Five Great Gift-Buying Strategies

1. **Buy it when you find it.** This means that when you happen across something that's exactly right for Dad's next birthday, buy it immediately. Don't say to yourself, "Oh, I'll come back for it next week." You won't. Buy it now, stash it away, and you'll have it when you need it.

2. **Buy it wherever you are.** If you happen to be far from home and you see that perfect bracelet for your sister, buy it and bring it back with you—it won't take up much room in your suitcase. Even if it's months later when you

give it to her, Sis will be thrilled you thought of her while you were on your vacation in Acapulco.

3. **Buy two.** If it's a great gift, there are at least two people on your list who will love it. Twice the results with half the work.

4. **Stay loose.** If you have too rigid or specific an idea about what you want to buy for Mom, you may overlook that perfect sweater as you race full speed ahead toward the silk scarves.

5. **Listen and learn.** If you're shopping with another person—wife, husband, child, friend—pay attention to what she or he oohs and aahs over. That's your next gift for her or him.

Gifts for Getting Organized

These may not be the most romantic gifts in the world, but they sure are useful for the organizationally challenged, the sort-of organized, and the superorganized alike. If the gift makes the desk, office, kitchen, or closet easier to deal with, it will be welcome.

Book on how to get organized

Homemade coupons for help with organizing—give these only if you're a champion organizer yourself! It's a good idea to make each coupon worth a two- or three-hour unit of help, so the disorganized giftee doesn't get overwhelmed by having to work at the task for too long in one session.

Homemade coupons for help with clearing out and throwing away stuff in attic, garage, closets, etc.

Consultation with a professional closet organizer

GIFTS FOR GETTING ORGANIZED

Closet accessories: shoe organizer, hat rack, hanging garment bag, sweater bag, stacking boxes, sliding wire baskets, in-closet bureau, etc.

Padded satin or other beautiful hangers

Tailor's hangers—made of wood, for hanging suits, shirts, skirts, pants

Wardrobe valet—has a hanger for jacket, a rod for trousers, a place for shoes, etc.

Dresser valet

Roll-up jewelry case

Jewelry box

Zippered cosmetic bag—canvas, leather, mesh, ripstop, microfiber, etc.

Zippered pouches in a variety of sizes, for carrying or storing anything

Purse accessories: eyeglass case, PDA holder, cell-phone carrier, coin purse, wallet, makeup case, key ring

Cedar chest

Underbed storage container

Pretty storage boxes—choose inexpensive heavy cardboard boxes printed with attractive patterns, or more expensive boxes in wood, leather, rattan, or other material.

Storage container for gift wrap and ribbon—for an extra-special gift, fill the container with rolls of wrapping paper, ribbons, bows, gift tags, scissors, and tape.

Photo album or slide file

Videotape or CD storage—cabinet, box, basket, tower, etc.

Over-the-seat car storage, with pockets for cassettes or CDs, snacks, odds and ends

Desk accessory set, including letter box, notepad holder, pen cup, etc.

GIFTS FOR GETTING ORGANIZED

Office Organizing Kit—put this together yourself. The kit might include file folders (manila or colored), expanding file and expanding envelopes, file labels, stacking boxes for the desk, pen cup, and desktop organizer with compartments for clips and other odds and ends.

Folding table for extra work surface— for crafts, sewing, paperwork, etc.

Sewing organizer, with drawers, compartments, thread storage

Bathroom organizers: tissue holder; containers for cosmetics, toiletries, cotton balls, soaps; over-the-door hook rack; tub caddy; shower caddy

GIFTS FOR GETTING ORGANIZED

Kitchen organizers: corner shelf, wire rack, drawer organizer, pot-and-pan lid organizer, sliding storage basket, cabinet organizer, etc.

Storage container for china, glassware, flatware, or silver

Kitchen canisters

Spice rack

Wood or bamboo dish rack

Nested mixing bowls in glass or stainless steel

Wine rack

Shopping cart

Week, month, or year's supply of something that's both nonperishable and gets used up regularly—this can be a rather surprising present but a tremendously thoughtful one. Be sure there's storage space for the gift (or you'll defeat the organizing purpose), and do package or wrap it in a cheerful way, to take a bit of the down-to-earth practicality out of it.

Here are some suggestions: paper napkins, tissues, or towels; toilet paper; plastic wrap and plastic bags; plastic containers; cleaning products; soap for bath, baby, dishes, or dishwasher; diapers; batteries; printer paper; pencils, pens, and markers; assorted tapes (transparent, masking, wrapping, etc.); stick-on notes; video- or audiocassettes; club soda or bottled water; cat or dog food.

Travel Gifts

Things that make travel more efficient, more manageable, more interesting, and more fun are terrific gifts indeed. And they celebrate one of life's greatest pleasures: vacations. They can also ease the trials of anyone who travels frequently for business, and that's no small matter. On this list you'll find everything for the plane, train, car, or armchair traveler.

TRAVEL GIFTS

Travel journal

Travel literature, such as memoir, fiction, history, ethnography, anthropology, book about a specific city or country

Book of photographs of a particular city, region, country, etc.

World atlas

Video documentary about a favorite country or a country to visit

Guidebook and map for a specific city or country

Restaurant guidebook

Tickets to a travel lecture

TRAVEL GIFTS

Language lessons or tapes

Handheld electronic language interpreter with words and phrases, currency conversions, etc.

Travel-size Scrabble or chess set

Travel-size packets of essentials—this might include toothpaste, mouthwash, soap, shampoo, conditioner, talcum powder, moisturizer, antiseptic cream, and more.

Compact manicure set

Toiletry kit with leakproof lining

Roll-up jewelry case

TRAVEL GIFTS

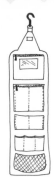

Hang-up-style personal
organizer with pouches,
zippered pockets, etc.

Microfiber waist pack

Weekender bag—
choose something with style.

Duffel bag—large for weekend trips,
extra large for longer trips

Roll-on luggage—often called a
"wheelie"

Carry-on garment bag

Leather luggage tags

Limo ride to the airport

TRAVEL GIFTS

Leather passport wallet

Wallet containing some appropriate currency for a planned trip

Neck wallet (also called neck pouch)—hangs from a cord or chain around the neck

Protective case (padded or molded) for cell phone, PDA, GPS unit, etc.

First-aid kit

Lightweight bathrobe

Warm foldable slippers

Packable clothing—you might choose a microfleece sweater or sleepwear, microfiber blazer or pants, microfiber raincoat, wrinkle-resistant silk jersey pullover or cardigan, silk jersey underwear, soft wool shawl, crushable hat in a bright color, and so on.

Photojournalist vest—with loads of pockets and pouches for stashing everything from passports to paperbacks

Waterproof zip-up jacket with removable liner

Raincoat with removable liner

Compact folding umbrella

Travel pillow

TRAVEL GIFTS

Travel clock with alarm

Travel radio with alarm, timer, etc.

Travel clock radio–CD player

Pocket-size shortwave radio

Tiny flashlight with long-lasting battery

Electrical converter kit (for using U.S. appliances in foreign countries)

Miniature hair dryer

Travel mirror

Champagne for a "bon voyage" toast

The Obligatory Gift

Into every life the necessity for giving an obligatory gift or two (or ten) must fall. Your whiny brother-in-law, the uncle you haven't seen in years, the friend who sends you something every Christmas when you wish she'd just forget the whole thing—there they are when the next Christmas or birthday or other gift-sensitive occasion rolls around.

The trick is to give the obligatory gift with a willing heart. You do *not* have to love the recipient or even like him, but you *do* have to accept the necessity of giving, as well as the true nature of giv-ing. You must force yourself to scrape up some generosity of spirit and do the thing properly. Not extravagantly, mind you, but properly. Though you may have to grit your teeth, pick something small but nice for Aunt Priscilla Snarly, and hope that in the fullness of time your generosity will have a salubrious effect on her character. It probably won't, but even if it doesn't, well, at least *you'll* have nothing to be ashamed of.

Special-Interest Gifts

It's a snap to choose a present for someone with a special interest: Simply give whatever he or she needs (or would love to have) for following that hobby or passion even further. If you're not sure what's needed, ask the giftee's best friend, mate, or kids.

◆ TIP ◆

In this section you'll find lists for three very common special interests, but of course there are dozens more—some of which you'll find in other sections, such as sports, fitness, cooking, crafts, and so on.

Gardener

Subscription to gardening magazine

Gardening book—planner, how-to, memoir, book of photographs (of country gardens, famous gardens, topiary, rock gardens, etc.)

Gardener's journal

High-quality tools—weeder, trowel, cultivator, rake, loppers, scissors, pruner

SPECIAL-INTEREST GIFTS

Cordless trimmer for grass or pruning

Electric hedge trimmer

Lawn mower

Leaf shredder

Garden cart or wheelbarrow

Outdoor or indoor composter

Freestanding outdoor greenhouse or shed

Greenhouse thermometer

Greenhouse heater

Bulbs, seeds, seedling starter kit

SPECIAL-INTEREST GIFTS

Pots of herbs

Bonsai tree and tools

Tomato ladders

Weatherproof markers

Birdhouse

Bird feeder

Hummingbird feeder

Birdbath

Sundial

Hammock

SPECIAL-INTEREST GIFTS

Garden chair

Garden chimes

Terra-cotta plant pots and saucers

Ceramic planters—lots of shapes, sizes, and glazes available

Straw or crocheted sun hat

Knee pads or padded kneeler

Waterproof outdoor clogs

Muck boots or shoes

Potting gloves

Botanical print in a nice frame

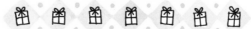

Driver or Car Enthusiast

Subscription to car magazine

Book about vintage cars or about a particular favorite car

Book on audiotape—for passing the time while driving

Audio system

CD storage sleeve that attaches to the visor

Hands-free phone

Commuter's mug

Driving gloves

SPECIAL-INTEREST GIFTS

Mechanic's gloves and coverall

Car and wheel brushes, duster brush

Handheld mini vacuum

Electric waxer and wax

Six months of car washes—by you or at a professional car wash

Seat cushion

Digital compass

Road maps

Roadside emergency kit

Trip to a car rally

Trip to an important race

Die-cast model car

Storage and organizing containers for the garage

Wine Lover

Subscription to wine connoisseur's newsletter or magazine

Book on wine—encyclopedia, wine-making how-to, memoir, study of wines of a particular region or country, etc.

Wine journal

Videotape about viticulture, wine tasting, serving wine, cooking with wine, etc.

SPECIAL-INTEREST GIFTS

Software about wine

Case of wine

Wine rack

Wine or champagne chiller

Thermometer

Battery-operated (or other) corkscrew

Cork puller

Wineglasses

Glass charms or tags

Decanter

Bottle tags, stoppers, coasters

SPECIAL-INTEREST GIFTS

Drip collars

Wine cradle

Single or double wine tote

Wine picnic basket

Poster, print, or painting of wine region, vineyard, or other wine-related theme

Stash-and-Store Last-Minute Gifts

Let's face it. There will inevitably be an occasion when you have to give a gift and you have no time to shop for it, much less choose it carefully. For this reason you must buy a few simple (almost generic) presents and stash them in a closet so you have them when you need them. Remember: Sometimes it's better to give a last-minute-but-perfectly-nice gift than no gift at all.

◆ TIP ◆

Package the present in a box
if at all possible—that makes it
look a lot less last-minute.

Boxes of note cards—stock up on a few boxes of simple but attractive folded note cards with matching envelopes. Museum cards are a good choice, but you could also pick blank cards made of elegant paper, cards printed or embossed with a simple design, or cards produced by an organization you support.

Box of three floral- or herbal-scented soaps

Tote bag made of white or natural cotton canvas, with brightly colored straps

STASH-AND-STORE LAST-MINUTE GIFTS

Bottle of good sherry

Solid-colored silk scarf, square or oblong

Knitted gloves

Earmuffs

Knitted watch cap

Baseball cap

Wool or wool-blend scarf in navy blue, gray, black, or hunter green

Plain but good quality T-shirts—small, medium, and large; in black, navy, and red

Leather wallet, change purse, eyeglass case

STASH-AND-STORE LAST-MINUTE GIFTS

Box of four or six champagne flutes

Two or four white or solid-color mugs

Three or more pretty dish towels

Clear glass bud vase

White or ivory candles—a dozen tapers or three pillars

Classic games—Monopoly, checkers, Scrabble, Candy Land, etc.

Slinky toy

Big box of crayons, plus a package of white construction paper

Small stuffed animal

STASH-AND-STORE LAST-MINUTE GIFTS

Pull toy

Classic children's book

Set of poster paints, plus a pair of brushes

Fancy yo-yo

Mini model car or other vehicle

The Best Gifts I Ever Got

When I was small, my parents didn't have much money. That wasn't something I understood very well, so I never expected Christmas to be anything but bountiful. On Christmas Day of the year I had just turned eight and my brother, Johnny, was four, I ran downstairs with high hopes—and I was not disappointed. There in the living room was the most amazing contraption I'd ever seen: My father, an engineer with a gift for carpentry, had built a child-size store for Johnny and me. It was a sort of countertop with shelves below and a sign above. There was a toy cash register (filled with pennies and play money) on the counter, little boxes and cans of food on the shelves, and the whole "store" (see the drawing below) rolled on wheels so we could push it to any room of the house. It was painted shiny white, and the lettering on the sign was bright green and red.

But that wasn't all I found under the tree. My mother, a housewife with a talent for sewing, handed me a big box tied with pink ribbon. Inside was a pale pink leotard, a pair of pink ballet slippers—and the most beautiful tutu in the entire world, a confection of many layers of pale pink netting dotted with silver glitter. To go with it there was a silver crown fit for a princess.

No little girl has ever had a more wonderful pair of presents, and to this day I remember with perfect clarity those gifts and the love with which they were made.

Do-It-Yourself Gifts

From the doily your great-aunt Harriet Speedyhook crochets for you to the basket of spa treats you put together for Sally Dearfriend, gifts created by loving hands are the most special gifts of all. They express your kind and caring thoughts even when they don't cost much money to make. And keep in mind that ingenuity can be as effective a special skill as crocheting or knitting when you're creating a DIY gift—see the basket ideas that follow.

Put It Together Yourself

Here are a few ideas to inspire you, but feel free to customize each basket for the person or family receiving it. A box, shopping bag, tote bag, or even a shiny aluminum bucket will hold the goodies attractively if you prefer not to use a basket. Also, check other lists ("Gifts of Food," page 17; "Gifts for Looking and Feeling Attractive," page 33; "Presents for Babies and New Moms and Dads," page 153; "Gifts for the Cook," page 217; etc.) for more ideas.

Beauty Basket: shampoo, styling gel, hairbrush, nail polish, lipstick, palette of eye shadows, eyelash curler, cosmetics case

Great-Feet-and-Legs Basket: foot cream, foot smoother, panty hose (sheer, in several colors), tights, knee-highs, knee socks, trouser socks, fun cotton socks, white crew socks

Spa Basket: bath salts, body lotion, facial mask, loofah, bottled water, small candy bar or energy bar, terry robe

Bon Voyage Basket: travel-size containers of shampoo, moisturizer, etc.; box of Ziploc bags; book of crossword puzzles; travel guide; tiny flashlight; tiny mending kit; packets of nuts, candy, mints; phone card

Breakfast Basket: coffee, tea, pair of mugs, grapefruits, pancake mix, maple syrup, canned ham, biscuit mix, jam, honey

Christmas Treats: candy canes, chocolate Santa, Christmas cookies, fruitcake, mixed nuts, a few tree ornaments

Chocolate Basket: chocolate bars, fudge, chocolate mints, brownies, chocolate cookies, chocolate syrup, cocoa

Sunshine Basket: oranges, lemons, limes, tangerines, clementines, kumquats, fruit drops, dried pineapple

Treat Basket: caramel popcorn, peanuts, pretzels, licorice, gummy bears, malted milk balls, lollipops, nonpareils, other candies

Crunch-and-Munch Basket: yellow tortilla chips, blue tortilla chips, mild and hot salsas, cheese crackers or cheese straws, roasted almonds, peanut brittle, pretzels, party mix

Fruit Fun Basket: Glacé apricots, peaches, and pears; clementine or mandarin oranges; chocolate-covered cherries; banana chips; strawberry and raspberry jam

Apple-and-Cheese Basket: two kinds of cheese (one sharp, one mild), two kinds of crackers, cheese straws, lady apples, variety of other apples

Herbs-and-Spices Basket: jars of dried herbs and spices, whole spices (cinnamon sticks, nutmeg), curry powder, peppercorns, pepper grinder, pots of fresh herbs (basil, parsley, rosemary, oregano, etc.)

Cook It Yourself

Pot of hearty soup

Dinners or main courses to be stashed in the freezer

Fresh bread

DO-IT-YOURSELF GIFTS

Muffins

Brownies

Cookies

Pound cake or Bundt cake

Decorated cupcakes

Fudge

Jam or preserves

Chutney or relish

Salsa—include chips in the package

DO-IT-YOURSELF GIFTS

Build It Yourself

Picture frame

Bookcase

Hope chest

Cradle

Dollhouse

Noah's ark and animals

Jigsaw puzzle

Children's playhouse

Garden shed

Doghouse

Birdhouse

Knit It Yourself

Simple pullover or cardigan

Cable-knit sweater

Fair Isle or other patterned sweater

Shawl

Scarf

Mittens or gloves

Hat or cap

Afghan

Baby blanket, booties, sweater, or
hooded bunting

Crochet It Yourself

Fancy doilies

Scarf

Hat or cap

Granny-square sweater or afghan

Lacy sweater

Triangular shawl or scarf

Baby sweater or blanket

Bedspread

Table runner

Tablecloth

Sew It Yourself

Doll clothes

Hand puppets

Child's party dress

Child's costume for Halloween or dress-up play

Beach cover-up

Kimono-style robe

Hostess skirt

Chef-style apron

Set of place mats and matching napkins

Patchwork quilt

Christmas stockings

Embroider It Yourself

Tea towels or guest towels

Place mats

Tablecloth and matching
napkins

Sampler, for framing

Baby dress

Baby bibs

Small zippered case

Tote bag

Decorative pillow

Pillowcases

Needlepoint It Yourself

Decorative pillow

Coasters

Chair seats

Cover for a footstool

Pincushion

Museum Gifts

Museum shops are invaluable resources for gift givers. Posters, books, jewelry, clothing, accessories, toys, games, ceramics, glass, folk art, postcards, stationery, videos—museum shops are treasure troves. Many large museums have on-line catalogs; most smaller museums don't. So browse the virtual sites by all means, but if you live near a small museum, be sure to take a trip over to it to check out the *actual* site.

Here are some Internet possibilities:

- ◆ Metropolitan Museum of Art: www.metmuseum.org/store
- ◆ Museum of Modern Art (New York): www.momastore.org
- ◆ Brooklyn Museum of Art: www.bmashop.com

- ◆ National Museum of Women Artists: www.nmwa.org/shop

- ◆ Museum of Fine Arts (Boston): www.mfa.org/shop
- ◆ Smithsonian Institution: www.smithsonianstore.com
- ◆ Museum of Contemporary Art (Los Angeles): www.moca-la.org/store
- ◆ Museum of New Mexico: www.shopmuseum.com
- ◆ Walker Art Center (Minneapolis): www.walkerart.org/shop
- ◆ Mystic Seaport Museum: www.mysticseaport.org/shop
- ◆ Heard Museum (Phoenix): www.heard.org/shop
- ◆ Dallas Museum of Art: www.store.yahoo.com/dallasmuseumofart
- ◆ Cleveland Museum of Art: www.clevelandart.org/store
- ◆ Philadelphia Museum of Art: www.store.yahoo.com/pma-store

Just-Because Gifts

A just-because gift is something you give just because you feel like giving it—on no special occasion, with no feeling of obligation, for no particular reason. In fact, you give it just because you want to make someone happy. Lovers often give each other just-because gifts, but *anyone* can give a just-because gift to anyone else. It can be a conventional present, of course, but sometimes a just-because gift takes a more whimsical or unexpected form. Serendipity plays a part, too: You're shopping downtown and you see a scarf that reminds you unequivocally of your niece Delilah Dresswell, so you buy it and give it to her—just because.

Bouquet of balloons sent to the office

Bouquet of wildflowers, picked by you

Orchid corsage

Shopping bag full of Hershey's Kisses

Book of love poetry—or any other kind of poetry

JUST-BECAUSE GIFTS

Book of fairy tales or a favorite children's book—for a grown-up

Book he's been longing for

Something she happened to mention she wanted

Something she's wanted all her life

Something for which he's been putting money aside

Something he'd never buy for himself

Love letter

Friendship ring

Chocolate bunny

Champagne and caviar

Lunch at a special restaurant

Home-cooked dinner of all his favorite foods

Batch of her favorite cookies

Giant tub of popcorn

Tickets to the circus

Trip to the zoo

Stuffed animal

Charm for her charm bracelet

Pearl for her add-a-pearl necklace

JUST-BECAUSE GIFTS

Diving lessons

Flying lessons

Tango lessons

Limousine pickup at the airport

Red sports car—rented for the weekend

A rose for each year you've been together

Twenty "LOVE" stamps from the post office

A calligraphic list of ten reasons why you love, like, or admire him or her

One new CD every month for a year

JUST-BECAUSE GIFTS

Stationery with her name and address printed on it

Labels with his name and address printed on them

Beautifully bound blank book

Box of colored pencils

Full-size poster of a favorite movie—and the video or DVD of the same movie

Framed autographed photo of a favorite personality—TV or sports celeb, movie or music star, literary or political figure

Surprise party for your sweetheart, parent, or dear friend

Phone call to say, "Hi, I'm thinking of you."